MorningStar
FARMS

The
Veggie Burger
Cookbook

FOG CITY PRESS

The Veggie Burger Cookbook

MorningStar FARMS®

How to Prepare Veggie Burgers

Veggie burgers from *Morningstar Farms* are quick and easy to make. Recipes in this book that combine and cook the burgers creatively with other ingredients provide specific instructions for how to prepare them. In general, however, follow cooking instructions given on the packages of the burgers you buy—along with the following basic guidelines.

GENERAL PREPARATION INSTRUCTIONS:

- Keep veggie burgers frozen until ready to use.
- Cook burgers thoroughly.
- For food safety and quality, whatever cooking method you use, always heat veggie burger patties to a minimum internal temperature of 160°F, using an instant-read thermometer *(right)* to test for doneness.

IN THE OVEN *(recommended method):*

- Preheat oven to 375°F.
- Place frozen burgers on a baking sheet and bake for 17 to 19 minutes, turning burgers over halfway through the cooking time.

ON THE GRILL

- Keep veggie burgers frozen until ready to use.
- Never leave grill unattended while in use.
- Children should be supervised.
- For food safety and quality, heat burgers to a minimum internal temperature of 160°F.
- The following instructions were developed using a gas grill. Grill performance may vary. Always follow manufacturer's instructions.
  1. Preheat the grill to medium-high heat.
  2. Remove frozen veggie burger patties from package.
  3. Lightly spray both sides of patties with cooking spray *(top right)*.
  4. Place patties on grill. Cover grill and cook for 3 minutes.
  5. Using a long-handled grill spatula, flip patties *(bottom right)*. Cover grill and cook for an additional 2½ minutes.
  6. Carefully insert tip of an instant-read thermometer into center of a patty. Watch reading carefully as it approaches desired minimum temperature of 160°F *(right)*.
  7. Use caution, as product will be hot. Carefully remove from grill.
  8. Cool briefly before serving.

IN THE SKILLET

- Thaw individual burgers by placing in microwave and heating on 50-percent power for 1 minute.
- Place thawed burgers in a nonstick skillet and cook over medium heat for 6 to 7 minutes, turning burgers frequently.

IN THE MICROWAVE

- Arrange frozen burgers on a microwaveable plate.
- Microwave on high setting, turning burgers over halfway through the cooking time (1 burger, 1 to 1½ minutes; 2 burgers, 2¼ to 3 minutes). Microwaving more than 2 burgers at one time is not recommended.
- Microwave ovens vary; times given are approximate.

Classic American Burgers

What could be more all-American than burgers with melted cheese, tomato, pickles and onion? Your favorite veggie burgers, plus reduced-fat cheese, turn the classic into a satisfying, healthful meal.

Preparation Time: 15 minutes | Total Time: 15 minutes | Servings: 2

2 *Morningstar Farms*
Grillers Prime Veggie Burgers

- or -

2 other *Morningstar Farms*
Veggie Burgers of your choice

2 slices (2 ounces total)
reduced-fat Cheddar, mozzarella,
or Swiss cheese *(see sidebar)*

2 leaves lettuce

2 hamburger buns, split and toasted

6 slices dill pickle

2 slices tomato

1 thin slice red onion,
separated into rings

Ketchup

Mustard

*For best results, see our tips
on pages 8-9.*

1. Cook burgers according to package directions. Immediately top each burger with one slice of cheese, if desired. Let stand for I minute to allow cheese to melt.

2. Place one lettuce leaf on each bun bottom. Top with burgers, pickles, tomato slices, onion rings, and bun tops. Serve with ketchup and mustard on the side.

ON THE GRILL: Preheat the grill. Use a food thermometer to be sure patties reach minimum internal temperature of I60°F.

NUTRITION FACTS: Serving Size: I Burger Sandwich; Calories: 370; Calories from Fat: I00; Total Fat: I2g; Saturated Fat: I.5g; Cholesterol: 0mg; Sodium: I030mg; Total Carbohydrates: 44g; Dietary Fiber: 6g; Sugars: 7g; Protein: 23g.

A Look at Reduced-fat Cheeses

If you love cheese but are trying to live more healthfully, reduced-fat versions of your favorite varieties offer the best of both worlds. Check the dairy aisle of your supermarket and you'll find a wide range of brands that offer Cheddar, Swiss, mozzarella, and other popular cheeses—many presliced or preshredded for easy use—with at least 25 percent of the fat removed. Try several different kinds on your veggie burgers, whether served as sandwiches or bunless *(right)*, until you find those you like the best.

Texas-style BBQ Burgers

Bottled barbecue sauce and relish, both available in the supermarket condiments aisle, turn veggie burgers into a down-home delight. If you want to reduce the fat, consider using low-fat cheese (page 10).

Preparation Time: 10 minutes | Total Time: 20 minutes | Servings: 2

2 *Morningstar Farms Grillers Prime* Veggie Burgers

- or -

2 other *Morningstar Farms* Veggie Burgers of your choice

2 slices (about 1½ ounces total) Cheddar cheese

2 hamburger buns, split

4 teaspoons barbecue sauce

4 teaspoons sweet pickle relish

2 slices onion, separated into rings

For best results, see our tips on pages 8-9.

1. Cook burgers according to package directions. Top each hot burger with cheese slice. Let stand until cheese melts, about 1 minute.

2. Serve burgers on buns along with barbecue sauce, relish, and onion.

ON THE GRILL: Preheat the grill. Use a food thermometer to be sure patties reach minimum internal temperature of 160°F.

NUTRITION FACTS: Serving Size: 1 Burger Sandwich; Calories: 410; Calories from Fat: 160; Total Fat: 18g; Saturated Fat: 6g; Cholesterol: 25mg; Sodium: 940mg; Total Carbohydrates: 35g; Dietary Fiber: 4g; Sugars: 10g; Protein: 26g.

Adding Southwestern Spice

Your supermarket condiments aisle will probably offer a wide array of bottled barbecue sauce choices, both national and regional brands, for the recipe above. Before you buy, read the label, paying close attention to the ingredients list—which always lists items in descending order of weight—and the nutrition data. Or, spice things up another popular Southwestern way, by topping burgers with strips of canned mild green roasted chilies and a spoonful of tomato salsa *(right)*.

Grillers Prime with Red Onion Jam

Slowly cooking onion intensifies the flavor of its natural sugars. When cooking the jam for this recipe, or even simple sautéed onions (see sidebar), watch carefully and stir frequently to avoid burning.

Preparation Time: 30 minutes I Total Time: 30 minutes I Servings: 4

1 red onion, peeled

1 cup water

3 tablespoons margarine or butter

1 tablespoon sugar

½ teaspoon salt

2 sprigs tarragon, leaves removed and finely chopped

3 tablespoons mayonnaise

3 tablespoons Dijon mustard

4 round sandwich rolls, split

8 large spinach leaves, thoroughly rinsed and patted dry

1 package *Morningstar Farms Grillers Prime* Veggie Burgers

   - or -

4 other *Morningstar Farms* Veggie Burgers of your choice

For best results, see our tips on pages 8-9.

1. Cut onion into slices ¼ inch thick. In saucepan, combine water, margarine, sugar, and salt. Bring to a boil over high heat and add onion slices. Continue boiling, stirring frequently, until most of water is evaporated. Reduce heat and simmer, stirring frequently, until mixture is thick like a jam. Set aside.

2. In small mixing bowl, stir together chopped tarragon, mayonnaise, and mustard. Spread on top and bottom of each roll. Place 2 spinach leaves on each roll. Set aside.

3. Prepare burgers according to package directions. Place a burger on each roll. Top each burger with red onion jam. Serve immediately.

NUTRITION FACTS: Serving Size: I Burger Sandwich; Calories: 500; Calories from Fat: 210; Total Fat: 24g; Saturated Fat: 6g; Cholesterol: 5mg; Sodium: 1350mg; Total Carbohydrates: 51g; Dietary Fiber: 6g; Sugars: 13g; Protein: 23g.

For Onion Lovers

If you love the sweet flavor of cooked onions on a burger, try another topping for your veggie burgers of choice. In a nonstick skillet over medium-low heat, melt I tablespoon margarine or butter. Add ¾ cup thinly sliced sweet onion (such as Vidalia, Maui, or Walla Walla) and cook, stirring frequently, until lightly browned, 14 to 18 minutes. If you like, stir in ½ teaspoon whole caraway seeds. Cook veggie burgers according to package directions. Serve them with buns or bunless, topped with cheese if you like. Spoon the sautéed onions on top and pass condiments to add to taste. Makes enough onions for 4 servings.

Garden Veggie Deluxe Burgers

A touch of curry powder from your market's seasonings aisle adds luxuriously intriguing flavor to these easy veggie burgers.

Preparation Time: 5 minutes | Total Time: 25 minutes | Servings: 2

2 *Morningstar Farms* Garden Veggie Patties Veggie Burgers

 - or -

2 other *Morningstar Farms* Veggie Burgers of your choice

2 slices (about 1½ ounces total) provolone cheese

2 tablespoons reduced-fat mayonnaise or regular mayonnaise

¼ teaspoon curry powder

2 whole-wheat hamburger buns, split

2 slices tomato

2 slices red onion

4 rings green or red bell pepper

Fresh flat-leaf parsley leaves, for garnish (optional)

For best results, see our tips on pages 8-9.

1. Cook burgers according to package directions. Top hot burgers with cheese slices. Let stand until cheese melts, about I minute.

2. Meanwhile, in small bowl, stir together mayonnaise and curry powder. Spread on bun bottoms. Top with burgers, tomato, red onion, and bell pepper. Top with parsley leaves, if you like, and bun tops.

ON THE GRILL: Preheat the grill. Use a food thermometer to be sure patties reach minimum internal temperature of 160°F.

NUTRITION FACTS: Serving Size: I Burger Sandwich; Calories: 410; Calories from Fat: 120; Total Fat: 13g; Saturated Fat: 5g; Cholesterol: 25mg; Sodium: 1090mg; Total Carbohydrates: 53g; Dietary Fiber: 8g; Sugars: 10g; Protein: 23g.

Garnishing with Fresh Herbs

Sprigs or leaves of fresh herbs make wonderfully flavorful, refreshing garnishes for veggie burgers. Look in your supermarket for widely available flat-leaf parsley *(see photo, opposite page)*. Or look for other options, including delicate fresh chervil, which tastes like mild parsley with a hint of anise; spicy fresh cilantro; basil leaves; or the peppery, slightly bitter herb arugula, shown at right beneath a chicken-flavored veggie burger patty.

Steakhouse Patty Melt

Enjoy all the satisfaction of a steakhouse and diner classic with your favorite veggie burger. Feel free to vary the recipe with different sautéed vegetables or another kind of cheese.

Preparation Time: 20 minutes | Total Time: 20 minutes | Servings: 2

4 teaspoons unsalted butter or margarine, softened

1 cup thinly sliced red onion

1 cup sliced fresh mushrooms

2 *Morningstar Farms Grillers Prime* Veggie Burgers

- or -

2 other *Morningstar Farms* Veggie Burgers of your choice

4 slices marble rye bread

1 tablespoon good-quality bottled steak sauce

2 slices Swiss cheese (2 ounces total)

For best results, see our tips on pages 8-9.

1. In large nonstick skillet, melt 2 teaspoons butter over medium-low heat. Add onion. Cook uncovered, stirring occasionally, until onion is tender and beginning to brown, about 10 minutes. Add mushrooms to onion. Cook, stirring occasionally, over medium-low heat until mushrooms are tender, 3 to 4 minutes more. Remove from skillet. Keep warm.

2. Add burgers to same skillet. Raise the heat to medium and cook, uncovered, until heated through, 7 to 8 minutes, turning once. Remove from skillet. Keep warm.

3. Remove skillet from heat. Carefully wipe out skillet with paper towel. Lightly spread remaining butter on one side of each bread slice. Place 2 bread slices, buttered side down, in skillet. Top with burgers, steak sauce, onion mixture, and cheese. Place remaining bread slices, buttered side up, on top. Cook, covered, over medium-low heat for 2 to 4 minutes or until golden brown on bottoms. Turn *(see sidebar, below)*. Cook, uncovered, until cheese melts and bread is golden brown, 2 to 3 minutes more. With spatula, transfer sandwiches to cutting board. Cut in half with sharp knife. Serve immediately.

ON THE GRILL: Preheat the grill. Use a food thermometer to make sure patties reach minimum internal temperature of 160°F.

NUTRITION FACTS: Serving Size: I Patty Melt; Calories: 550; Calories from Fat: 260; Total Fat: 28g; Saturated Fat: 12g; Cholesterol: 50mg; Sodium: 910mg; Total Carbohydrates: 44g; Dietary Fiber: 7g; Sugars: 11g; Protein: 31g.

A Two-Handed Trick for Easy Patty Melts

A diner favorite, patty melts are easy to make at home—until, that is, some cooks try to flip the sandwiches over in the skillet only to have them fall apart before the cheese has melted completely. Using a pair of spatulas, however, makes turning the sandwiches easy. Just slip one spatula underneath the sandwich and, with your other hand, press down on the top with another spatula to clamp the sandwich firmly *(left)*. Lift the sandwich slightly, rotate your wrists together to turn it over, and slide it back into the skillet to finish cooking.

Cajun Black 'n' Blue Burgers

Cajun cooking often features lively spice blends, sometimes called blackening spices because they are rubbed on foods before searing to a dark, tasty finish. Here, they season veggie burgers that also gain big flavor from crumbled blue cheese.

Preparation Time: 10 minutes | Total Time: 20 minutes | Servings: 2

2 *Morningstar Farms Grillers Prime* Veggie Burgers

- or -

2 other *Morningstar Farms* Veggie Burgers of your choice

¼ teaspoon Cajun seasoning

2 slices red onion, separated into rings

2 lettuce leaves

2 hamburger buns or Kaiser rolls, split

2 slices tomato

2 tablespoons crumbled blue cheese

For best results, see our tips on pages 8-9.

1. Preheat oven to 350°F. Place burgers on baking sheet. Bake for 8 minutes. Turn burgers. Sprinkle with Cajun seasoning. Bake until heated through, 7 to 8 minutes more.

2. Meanwhile, in small nonstick skillet coated with cooking spray, cook onion over medium-low heat until tender, stirring frequently, about 5 minutes.

3. Place lettuce leaves on bun bottoms. Top with burgers, tomato slices, onion rings, blue cheese, and bun tops.

ON THE GRILL: Preheat the grill. Use a food thermometer to be sure patties reach minimum internal temperature of l60°F.

NUTRITION FACTS: Serving Size: I Burger Sandwich; Calories: 340; Calories from Fat: l20; Total Fat: l4g; Saturated Fat: 3g; Cholesterol: 5mg; Sodium: 8l0mg; Total Carbohydrates: 32g; Dietary Fiber: 4g; Sugars: 6g; Protein: 22g.

Adding Bold Flavors to Veggie Burgers

Your favorite veggie burger has enough hearty flavor on its own to welcome and complement robust accompaniments. In addition to the combination of hot spices and tangy blue cheese in the burger above, look in your market for other seasonings, sauces, and spreads. The Middle Eastern-inspired flatbread-wrapped burgers shown here, for example, feature hummus, the popular spread of pureed chickpeas, sesame paste, garlic, and cumin, sold ready to use in the refrigerated case. A squeeze of fresh lemon adds the perfect finishing touch before eating.

Portobello Mushroom and Onion Burgers

A quickly prepared topping of the flavorful fresh mushrooms known as Portobellos or their smaller form, creminis, form the foundation of a robust addition to veggie burgers.

Preparation Time: 20 minutes I Total Time: 20 minutes I Servings: 4

4 ounces small Portobello or cremini mushrooms, stems trimmed, caps sliced

½ cup chopped onion

1 teaspoon olive oil

¼ cup water

¼ cup bottled steak sauce

4 *Morningstar Farms Grillers Prime* Veggie Burgers

- or -

4 *Morningstar Farms Grillers* Vegan Veggie Burgers

- or -

4 *Morningstar Farms Grillers* Original Veggie Burgers

4 hamburger buns

For best results, see our tips on pages 8-9.

1. In large saucepan, combine mushrooms, onion, and olive oil. Cook over medium heat, stirring constantly, for 3 to 4 minutes. Add water, cover pan, and simmer 3 to 4 minutes longer, until vegetables are tender. Remove lid and stir in steak sauce.

2. Prepare veggie burgers according to package directions.

3. Place burgers on bottom halves of buns. Spoon warm mushroom mixture on top. Serve immediately.

ON THE GRILL: Preheat the grill. Use a food thermometer to make sure patties reach minimum internal temperature of 160°F.

NUTRITION FACTS: Serving Size: I Burger Sandwich with topping; Calories: 330; Calories from Fat: 110; Total Fat: 12g; Saturated Fat: 1.5g; Cholesterol: 0mg; Sodium: 860mg; Total Carbohydrates: 32g; Dietary Fiber: 5g; Sugars: 5g; Protein: 21g.

Enjoying Hearty Mushroom Flavor

Lovers of vegetables know the rich, meaty flavor mushrooms can contribute to a main course. Quickly sautéed and turned into a juicy topping, as in the recipe above, they're a classic burger addition. Good-sized mushroom caps such as those from Portobellos, creminis, or regular cultivated mushrooms also make wonderful containers for stuffing *(right)*. Here, they're filled with a mixture of 6 ounces *Morningstar Farms Meal Starters* Recipe Crumbles (or use an equivalent weight of crumbled veggie burgers), ½ cup breadcrumbs, ½ cup shredded mozzarella cheese, ½ teaspoon each dried basil and oregano, and ¼ teaspoon garlic powder, then baked on a baking sheet coated with vegetable cooking spray in a 350°F oven until browned and bubbling-hot, about 15 minutes.

Burgers with Chunky Grilled Vegetables

Topped with a medley of quickly grilled, garlic-scented summer vegetables and drizzled with a tangy-sweet reduction of balsamic vinegar, these bunless veggie burgers become an elegantly casual main course.

Preparation Time: 20 minutes | Total Time: 20 minutes | Servings: 2

⅓ cup balsamic vinegar

2 teaspoons olive oil

1 teaspoon minced garlic

½ medium yellow bell pepper, stem, seeds, and white veins removed

½ medium red bell pepper, stem, seeds, and white veins removed

1 small zucchini, trimmed and halved lengthwise

1 baby eggplant or Japanese eggplant, trimmed and halved lengthwise

4 Morningstar Farms *Grillers* Original

  - or -

4 Morningstar Farms Grillers Vegan Veggie Burgers

For best results, see our tips on pages 8-9.

1. In small saucepan cook vinegar over low heat about 5 minutes or until reduced to 2 tablespoons and syrupy. Set aside.

2. In small bowl stir together olive oil and garlic. Brush bell peppers, zucchini, and eggplant with olive oil mixture.

3. Grill peppers and zucchini over medium heat for 5 minutes, turning occasionally. Add burgers and eggplant to grill. Grill for 4 to 6 minutes more or until burgers are heated through and vegetables are tender, turning occasionally. (Use an instant-read thermometer to make sure that the patties reach a minimum internal temperature of 160°F.) Remove from grill. Cut vegetables into slices ¾ to 1 inch thick.

4. To serve, spoon vegetables on burgers. Drizzle with balsamic vinegar.

ALTERNATIVE COOKING METHOD: The vegetables and burgers may also be cooked on an indoor grill or stovetop grill *(see below)*, under the broiler, or with a two-sided countertop electric contact grill. If using a contract grill, which cooks both sides at once, cut the cooking time by about half.

NUTRITION FACTS: Serving Size: 1 Burger + ½ Cup Vegetables (288 g); Calories: 250; Calories from Fat: 90; Total Fat: 10g; Saturated Fat: 1.5g; Cholesterol: 0mg; Sodium: 350mg; Total Carbohydrates: 28g; Dietary Fiber: 7g; Sugars: 15g; Protein: 16g.

Celebrate Summer Year-Round with Grilled Vegetables

The bell peppers, zucchini, and eggplant featured in this recipe are so-called "vegetable fruits," botanically classified as members of the fruit family because of the way they grow. All at their peak of season in summer, but available year-round, they have a natural sweetness that is highlighted by grilling. When the weather isn't friendly to outdoor grilling, try cooking them on a simple ridged stovetop grill *(left)*, keeping a close eye on the vegetables and turning them with tongs as soon as they start to become tender and are marked by the grill's ridges.

Spicy Tex-Mex Pita Burgers

Whole-wheat pita bread halves (see sidebar) *make fun, convenient containers for a Southwestern-style combination of veggie burgers, greens, avocado, salsa, and a sprinkling of jalapeño pepper-spiked cheese.*

Preparation Time: 20 minutes I Total Time: 20 minutes I Servings: 2

2 *Morningstar Farms*
Spicy Black Bean Veggie Burgers

 - or -

2 other *Morningstar Farms*
Veggie Burgers of your choice

1 cup baby romaine lettuce or
torn romaine lettuce

2 tablespoons reduced-fat
mayonnaise

4 teaspoons chopped fresh cilantro

½ medium avocado, pitted,
peeled, chopped

4 tablespoons tomato salsa

1 whole-wheat pita bread round

4 tablespoons shredded Cheddar
cheese with jalapeño peppers
or Monterey Jack cheese with
jalapeño peppers

10 baked tortilla chips (optional)

*For best results, see our tips
on pages 8-9.*

1. Cook burgers according to package directions.

2. Meanwhile, in mixing bowl, toss together lettuce, mayonnaise, and cilantro until lettuce is evenly coated. In another bowl, stir together avocado and salsa.

3. Cut pita bread across middle in half. Fill each half with lettuce mixture. Insert burgers. Add cheese and avocado mixture. Serve with tortilla chips, if desired.

NUTRITION FACTS: Serving Size: ½ Pita; Calories: 430; Calories from Fat: 160; Total Fat: 17g; Saturated Fat: 5g; Cholesterol: 20mg; Sodium: 980mg; Total Carbohydrates: 51g; Dietary Fiber: 12g; Sugars: 5g; Protein: 21g.

Using Pita for Veggie Burgers

If you're trying to cut calories and carbohydrates, consider substituting pita bread for the usual burger buns. Half a whole-wheat pita round, big enough to hold a veggie burger patty and all the trimmings, has almost half the calories and carbs of a standard hamburger bun, and more than twice the fiber. To use a pita, simply cut it in half across its diameter with a sharp knife. With your fingertips, carefully open up each pita half into a pocket along the cut edge and then insert the veggie burger *(right)* and other sandwich fillings.

Italian Burgers with Bell Peppers

A quick sauté of bell peppers, onion, and a store-bought Italian seasoning blend brings authentic Mediterranean style to veggie burgers. Try other Italian-inspired variations as well (see sidebar).

Preparation Time: 20 minutes | Total Time: 20 minutes | Servings: 4

4 *Morningstar Farms* Tomato & Basil Pizza Burgers

- or -

4 *Morningstar Farms* Zesty Tomato Basil Burgers made with Organic Soy

- or -

4 other *Morningstar Farms* Veggie Burgers of your choice

¼ cup bottled herb pasta sauce

4 thin slices (about 3 ounces total) Provolone cheese (about 3 ounces total)

1 teaspoon olive oil

½ medium red bell pepper, cut into ¼-inch-wide strips

½ medium green bell pepper, cut into ¼-inch-wide strips

¼ large sweet onion, cut into slivers

½ teaspoon dried Italian seasoning

4 hamburger buns, split and toasted

For best results, see our tips on pages 8-9.

1. Preheat oven to 350°F. Place burgers on baking sheet. Bake for 11 minutes. Spread with pasta sauce. Top with cheese. Continue baking until cheese melts, about 3 minutes more.

2. Meanwhile, heat olive oil in large nonstick skillet over medium-high heat. Add red pepper, green pepper, onion, and Italian seasoning and cook, stirring frequently, until vegetables are tender.

3. With spatula, transfer cheese-topped burgers to bun bottoms. Spoon pepper mixture on top, add bun tops, and serve.

NUTRITION FACTS: Serving Size: I Burger Sandwich plus ½ Cup Pepper Mixture; Calories: 360; Calories from Fat: I40; Total Fat: 15g; Saturated Fat: 5g; Cholesterol: 20mg; Sodium: 730mg; Total Carbohydrates: 34g; Dietary Fiber: 6g; Sugars: 9g; Protein: 22g.

More Sources of Italian Inspiration

Your supermarket makes it easy to get creative making other Italian-style veggie burgers. Look in the refrigerated case for ready-to-use basil pesto sauce to stir into reduced-fat or regular mayonnaise. Find jars of roasted red bell peppers in the pickles and condiments aisle. Buy thinly sliced mozzarella or provolone cheese. Check the bakery section for Italian sourdough rolls or the pizza-style bread called focaccia. In the burger at right, all those ingredients—plus fresh basil leaves—come together to make a colorful sandwich packed with flavor.

Pollo Pomodoro Panini

The lilting Italian name translates simply as "chicken tomato sandwiches." Here, of course, chicken-flavored veggie burger patties provide the protein. Grilling the bread (see sidebar) adds an extra dimension.

Preparation Time: 15 minutes | Total Time: 25 minutes | Servings: 4

2 tablespoons finely shredded
or grated Parmesan cheese

2 tablespoons chopped fresh basil

2 cloves garlic, minced

4 slices firm-textured tomato,
each ¼ inch thick

1 piece focaccia, 8 to 9 inches
square, cut into fourths and split
horizontally, or 1 Italian ciabatta
loaf, cut into 8 slices

2 teaspoons olive oil

4 *Morningstar Farms
Chik Patties* Original

  - *or* -

4 other *Morningstar Farms
Chik Patties* Veggie Patties

  - *or* -

4 other *Morningstar Farms*
Veggie Burgers of your choice

4 slices (about 4 ounces total)
mozzarella cheese (optional)

1 cup prewashed
baby spinach leaves

*For best results, see our tips
on pages 8-9.*

1. In small bowl, combine Parmesan cheese, basil, and garlic. Sprinkle over one side of each tomato slice. Set aside.

2. Brush cut sides of focaccia with olive oil. Set aside.

3. Coat cold grill rack with nonstick coating. Preheat grill. Place patties on grill rack over medium heat. Grill for 6 minutes. Turn patties. Grill for 2 minutes more. Top each patty with cheese slice, if desired. Place tomato slices, Parmesan side up, and bread pieces, oil side down, alongside patties on grill rack. Grill about 2 minutes more or until cheese begins to melt and bread begins to brown.

4. Arrange spinach on half of the bread pieces. Top with patties, tomato slices, and remaining bread pieces. Serve immediately.

IN THE OVEN: Bake patties according to package directions. Top each with cheese, if desired, during the last minute of baking. Remove from oven. Keep warm. Place tomato slices, Parmesan side up, and bread pieces, oil side up, on shallow baking pan. Broil 4 inches from heat until cheese begins to melt and bread begins to brown, 3 to 4 minutes. Assemble sandwiches as directed above. Serve immediately.

NUTRITION FACTS: Serving Size: I Panini; Calories: 310; Calories from Fat: 90; Total Fat: 10g; Saturated Fat: 2g; Cholesterol: 0mg; Sodium: 860mg; Total Carbohydrates: 40g; Dietary Fiber: 4g; Sugars: 2g; Protein: 14g.

Grilling Veggie Burger Sandwich Bread

The rich flavor, crunchy texture, and golden-brown color that comes from grilling bread can enhance any veggie burger sandwich. In the recipe above, the bread is grilled on the outdoor grill. But you can also grill it easily on an indoor countertop grill or on a ridged cast-iron grill pan on the stovetop *(right)*. Be sure to watch carefully to avoid burning the bread, turning it as soon as it has grill marks.

Feta-Mint Burgers

The flavors of the eastern Mediterranean abound in these easy veggie burgers, which gain authentic personality from a quickly made sauce featuring fat-free yogurt (see sidebar), *crumbled feta cheese, and fresh mint.*

Preparation Time: 20 minutes | Total Time: 20 minutes | Servings: 4

4 *Morningstar Farms*
Zesty Tomato Basil Burgers
made with Organic Soy

  - *or* -

4 other *Morningstar Farms*
Veggie Burgers of your choice

4 hamburger buns,
split and toasted

⅓ cup crumbled feta cheese

2 tablespoons fat-free plain yogurt

1 tablespoon thinly sliced
fresh mint leaves

1 clove garlic, minced

1 medium tomato, thinly sliced

2 medium pepperoncini peppers,
sliced into rings

*For best results, see our tips
on pages 8-9.*

1. Cook burgers according to package directions.

2. Meanwhile, toast hamburger buns.

3. In small bowl, stir together cheese, yogurt, mint, and garlic.

4. Place burgers on bun bottoms. Top each burger with tomato slices, cheese-yogurt mixture, and pepperoncini peppers.

NUTRITION FACTS: Serving Size: I Burger Sandwich; Calories: 300; Calories from Fat: I00; Total Fat: IIg; Saturated Fat: 3.5g; Cholesterol: I0mg; Sodium: 850mg; Total Carbohydrates: 32g; Dietary Fiber: 6g; Sugars: 8g; Protein: I8g.

Yogurt Sauces for Veggie Burgers

Plain nonfat or low-fat yogurt forms the foundation for a wonderfully rich-tasting, tangy sauce for veggie burgers, whether served on buns or on their own. In addition to the sauce in the burger recipe above, try seasoning the yogurt with other herbs or spices, as well as finely chopped fresh vegetables. For an Indian-style sauce known as raita *(right)*, enough for 4 burgers, stir together ¼ cup yogurt, ½ cup finely chopped seeded cucumber, ¼ cup finely chopped red onion, ¼ teaspoon ground cumin, ⅛ teaspoon garlic powder, and ⅛ teaspoon salt.

Caribbean Jerk Burgers

The Caribbean seasoning called "jerk," which includes such spices as cayenne, allspice, cinnamon, and nutmeg, adds island magic to these intriguing bun-free burgers. An easy cabbage slaw helps cool things down.

Preparation Time: 5 minutes I Total Time: 25 minutes I Servings: 4

2 tablespoons reduced-calorie cole slaw dressing

2 tablespoons fat-free mayonnaise

1½ teaspoons Caribbean jerk seasoning

4 *Morningstar Farms Grillers* Vegan Veggie Burgers

- or -

4 *Morningstar Farms Grillers Prime* Veggie Burgers

- or -

4 other *Morningstar Farms* Veggie Burgers of your choice

¾ cup shredded green cabbage *(see sidebar)* or packaged cole slaw mix

¾ cup shredded red cabbage *(see sidebar)* or packaged cole slaw mix

For best results, see our tips on pages 8-9.

1. In mixing bowl, combine dressing, mayonnaise, and jerk seasoning. Set aside.

2. Place frozen burgers on baking sheet. Bake at 350°F for 10 minutes. Turn burgers. Spread half of jerk mixture on top of burgers. Bake 8 to 10 minutes more.

3. Add cabbages to bowl with remaining jerk mixture and toss well. Transfer burgers to serving plates. Top burgers with cabbage mixture and serve.

ON THE GRILL: Preheat the grill. After turning burgers, spread half of jerk mixture on top. Use a food thermometer to be sure patties reach minimum internal temperature of 160°F.

NUTRITION FACTS: Serving Size: 1 Burger plus ⅜ cup Cole Slaw; Calories: 130; Calories from Fat: 25; Total Fat: 3g; Saturated Fat: 0g; Cholesterol: 0mg; Sodium: 620mg; Total Carbohydrates: 10g; Dietary Fiber: 4g; Sugars: 2g; Protein: 13g.

Shredded Cabbage Made Easy

Many supermarket produce sections offer prepackaged shredded cole slaw mix. But it's easy to do it yourself, too, especially since some markets even sell halved or quartered cabbages, ready for you to start slicing. Just place a cabbage quarter on a cutting board with one cut side down, the other vertical. Starting about ⅛ inch or less in from the top edge of the cut side, and steadying the cabbage with your free hand while keeping fingertips safely clear, carefully use a sharp knife to cut a thin slice straight down *(right)*. Continue until you have enough slices, which separate easily into shreds.

Grilled Rustic Roll-ups

When the weather turns warm, fire up the grill to make these colorful, delicious country-style sandwiches featuring marinated seasonal vegetables and your veggie burgers of choice.

Preparation Time: 15 minutes | Total Time: 1 hour 30 minutes | Servings: 8

2 small yellow summer squash
(3 to 4 ounces each), trimmed

1 medium eggplant
(about 12 ounces), trimmed

3 onion slices, each about
½ inch thick

½ cup reduced-sodium soy sauce

½ cup orange juice

2 tablespoons olive oil
or vegetable oil

4 *Morningstar Farms* Garden
Veggie Patties Veggie Burgers

  - or -

4 *Morningstar Farms*
Spicy Black Bean Veggie Burgers

  - or -

4 other *Morningstar Farms*
Veggie Burgers of your choice

8 (9-inch) flour tortillas,
warmed *(see page 82)*

2 cups chopped romaine lettuce

½ cup shredded Monterey Jack
cheese with peppers
(about 2 ounces)

*For best results, see our tips
on pages 8-9.*

1. Cut each squash lengthwise into slices ³/₈ inch thick. Cut eggplant into 12 slices. Place squash, eggplant, and onion slices in large sealable plastic food bag. Drizzle with soy sauce, orange juice, and olive oil. Seal bag. Place in shallow pan. Refrigerate 1 to 12 hours, turning occasionally. Drain vegetables. Discard marinade.

2. Coat cold grill rack with nonstick coating. Preheat grill. Place burgers and onion slices on grill rack over medium heat. Grill for 3 minutes. Add eggplant slices to grill rack. Grill for 3 minutes more. Add squash slices to grill rack. Continue grilling until vegetables are tender and burgers are heated through to a minimum internal temperature of 160°F, 5 to 6 minutes longer, turning once.

3. Cut burgers into strips. Separate onion slices into rings. Cut eggplant slices into strips. Top tortillas with burger strips, onion rings, eggplant strips, lettuce, and cheese. Roll up. Cut each roll-up crosswise in half. Serve immediately.

NUTRITION FACTS: Serving Size: 1 Roll-up; Calories: 300; Calories from Fat: 90; Total Fat: 10g; Saturated Fat: 2.5g; Cholesterol: 5mg; Sodium: 1090mg; Total Carbohydrates: 40g; Dietary Fiber: 4g; Sugars: 6g; Protein: 13g.

Wrap and Roll-up Variations

Veggie burgers make it so easy to make all kinds of delicious wraps, roll-ups, and burritos *(see page 38)*. Just cook your favorite burgers, cut into strips, and wrap or roll them up in a flour tortilla of your choice—white, whole-wheat, or flavored with spinach or tomato—with other ingredients such as salad leaves, grilled vegetables, shredded cheese, avocado, sour cream, or whatever else you like. A Southwest Wrap *(right)*, for example, might include torn romaine, guacamole, salsa, and your favorite veggie burger, rolled up in a whole-wheat tortilla.

Chipotle Bean Burritos

Mexico's chipotle chili powder, made from smoke-dried jalapeño peppers, gives these robust burritos a satisfying but not-too-fiery heat. Canned pinto beans make preparation quick and easy; but, if you have some extra time and want to reduce the sodium in the recipe, consider cooking the beans yourself (see sidebar).

Preparation Time: 20 minutes | Total Time: 35 minutes | Servings: 6

6 (8-inch) flour tortillas

4 *Morningstar Farms*
Spicy Black Bean Veggie Burgers

- or -

4 other *Morningstar Farms*
Veggie Burgers of your choice

1 can (15 ounces) pinto beans,
rinsed and drained (see sidebar,
below)

½ cup sliced green onions,
plus extra for garnish

1⅓ cups salsa

½ teaspoon chipotle chili powder
or regular chili powder

1 cup shredded reduced-fat
Cheddar cheese (about 4 ounces)

3 cups sliced lettuce

⅓ cup fat-free sour cream

*For best results, see our tips
on pages 8-9.*

1. Tightly wrap tortillas in foil. Bake at 350°F until softened, about 7 minutes. Leave oven on. Meanwhile, cut veggie burgers into bite-sized pieces. Set aside.

2. Put rinsed and drained beans in mixing bowl. Use back of wooden spoon to slightly mash them. Stir in ½ cup green onions, ⅓ cup of the salsa, and chili powder. Spread bean mixture on each tortilla just below center. Sprinkle veggie burger pieces and cheese on top. Fold bottom edges of tortillas over filling. Fold in sides. Roll up. Secure with wooden toothpicks, if necessary.

3. On baking sheet coated with nonstick cooking spray or lined with parchment paper, place tortilla packages, seam side up. Bake until heated through and beginning to brown, about 15 minutes.

4. Arrange lettuce on 6 serving plates. Top with burritos, removing toothpicks if used. Spoon remaining salsa and sour cream alongside. Sprinkle with more green onion, if desired.

NUTRITION FACTS: Serving Size: 1 Burrito; Calories: 300; Calories from Fat: 70; Total Fat: 7g; Saturated Fat: 2g; Cholesterol: 5mg; Sodium: 1210mg; Total Carbohydrates: 40g; Dietary Fiber: 8g; Sugars: 6g; Protein: 19g.

Reducing Sodium By Cooking Your Own Beans

Canned beans, though convenient, can be high in sodium, and even those labeled low sodium can have approximately 125 mg in a ½-cup serving. To reduce sodium even further, cook your own dried beans instead. In medium saucepan, combine 3 cups water and ¾ cup sorted and rinsed dried pinto beans. Bring to full boil. Reduce heat. Simmer, uncovered, for 2 minutes. Remove from heat. Let stand, covered, for 1 hour. Drain. Rinse. Return beans to saucepan. Add 3 cups fresh water. Bring to boil. Reduce heat. Simmer, covered, until tender, 1 to 1½ hours. Drain. Use as directed above in recipe.

Spicy Black Bean Tacos

Cut any veggie burger in half and it fits perfectly into store-bought crispy taco shells for an easy Mexican treat.

Preparation Time: 10 minutes | Total Time: 20 minutes | Servings: 4

1 package *Morningstar Farms* Spicy Black Bean Veggie Burgers, thawed

- or -

4 other *Morningstar Farms* Veggie Burgers of your choice, thawed

8 ready-to-serve crispy taco shells

½ cup shredded fat-free Cheddar cheese

1 cup shredded lettuce

½ cup chopped tomato

½ cup fresh tomato salsa *(see sidebar)*

⅓ cup reduced-fat sour cream (optional)

For best results, see our tips on pages 8-9.

1. Preheat oven to 350°F.

2. Cut thawed veggie burgers in half. Place one half, cut side down, in each taco shell. Place taco shells on ungreased baking sheet.

3. Bake in preheated oven until burgers are hot and taco shells are toasted, about 7 minutes. Top each taco with cheese, lettuce, tomato, salsa, and sour cream. Serve immediately.

NUTRITION FACTS: Serving Size: 2 Tacos; Calories: 195; Calories from Fat: 30; Total Fat: 4g; Saturated Fat: 2g; Cholesterol: 10mg; Sodium: 910mg; Total Carbohydrates: 22g; Dietary Fiber: 6g; Sugars: 2g; Protein: 19g.

Making Your Own Fresh Salsa

Most supermarkets nowadays carry containers of fresh ready-to-serve tomato salsa in their refrigerated cases, and good-quality bottled tomato salsas are widely available, too. But nothing beats the flavor, and satisfaction, of making your own salsa from scratch. There's no secret formula. All you need for the most basic version are fresh ripe tomatoes, cut into small dice; minced fresh chilies such as medium-hot jalapeños *(right)*; and chopped fresh cilantro leaves. Add some finely minced onion if you like. Combine in whatever proportions suit your taste, using more tomato for milder, sweeter results, more chilies for hotter salsa. Season to taste with salt.

Spicy Thai Burgers

The bright yet soothing flavors of Thai cooking give veggie burgers an exotic, pleasing personality.

Preparation Time: 25 minutes | Total Time: 25 minutes | Servings: 4

1 cup fresh snow peas, trimmed

½ cup shredded carrots

½ cup quartered cherry tomatoes

⅓ cup sliced green onions

2 tablespoons slivered fresh
Thai basil or fresh basil

¼ cup unsweetened light coconut
milk or unsweetened coconut milk
(see sidebar)

1 tablespoon lime juice

½ teaspoon toasted Asian-style
sesame oil or toasted sesame seeds

¼ teaspoon crushed red
pepper flakes

4 *Morningstar Farms
Grillers Prime* Veggie Burgers

  - or -

4 other *Morningstar Farms*
Veggie Burgers of your choice

1 piece focaccia, 8 to 9 inches
square, cut into fourths and split
horizontally

*For best results, see our tips
on pages 8-9.*

1. Cut pea pods lengthwise into slivers. In medium bowl, toss together pea pods, carrots, tomatoes, green onions, and basil. Set aside.

2. In small bowl, whisk together coconut milk, lime juice, sesame oil, and red pepper flakes. Drizzle mixture over vegetables. Toss until vegetables are thoroughly coated.

3. Cook veggie burgers according to package directions.

4. Serve hot burgers in focaccia, topped with vegetable mixture.

ON THE GRILL: Preheat the grill. Use a food thermometer to be sure patties reach minimum internal temperature of 160°F.

NUTRITION FACTS: Serving Size: 1 Burger Sandwich; Calories: 330; Calories from Fat: 96; Total Fat: 11.5g; Saturated Fat: 2g; Cholesterol: 0mg; Sodium: 650mg; Total Carbohydrates: 31g; Dietary Fiber: 4g; Sugars: 0g; Protein: 23g.

Using Canned Coconut Milk

Coconut milk is a water-based extract of the rich-tasting, milky fat in the flesh of coconuts, not to be confused with the thin, clear coconut water inside coconuts. Not so long ago, cooks who wanted it had to crack open coconuts, grate them, and soak in hot water, then squeeze out the milk. Now, fortunately, many supermarkets carry canned coconut milk, usually in the Asian foods section. Sometimes, the rich "cream" of the coconut milk rises to form a thick layer at the top of the can. If your canned coconut milk has separated, place it in a mixing bowl. Stir briskly with a wire whisk *(right)* until smooth before measuring.

Asian-style Lettuce Wraps

When time is short and you crave Asian food, don't order take-out. Instead, in just 10 minutes you can whip together these simple lettuce wraps. They're sure to become a family favorite.

Preparation Time: 10 minutes | Total Time: 10 minutes | Servings: 8

¼ cup sliced green onion

4 *Morningstar Farms Grillers* Vegan Veggie Burgers, cut into strips

- or -

2 other *Morningstar Farms* Veggie Burgers of your choice, cut into strips

3 tablespoons reduced-sodium soy sauce

1 tablespoon cider vinegar

1 teaspoon ground ginger

⅛ teaspoon ground red pepper

2 cups packaged cole slaw mix or shredded cabbage *(see page 35)*

8 butterhead lettuce leaves or other leafy lettuce leaves

For best results, see our tips on pages 8-9.

1. In a nonstick skillet coated with vegetable cooking spray, cook the onion over medium heat for I minute. Stir in burger strips. Cook, stirring, until heated through.

2. In a small mixing bowl, stir together the soy sauce, vinegar, ginger, and red pepper. Add soy mixture and cole slaw mix to burger strips in skillet. Gently toss until combined and cabbage is slightly wilted, about I minute.

3. Spoon some burger mixture into each lettuce leaf. Wrap leaf around filling. Secure with wooden toothpick. Serve immediately, spooning any extra sauce left in the skillet into small cups to serve alongside for dipping.

NUTRITION FACTS: Serving Size: I Lettuce Wrap; Calories: 60; Calories from Fat: I0; Total Fat: Ig; Saturated Fat: 0g; Cholesterol: 0mg; Sodium: 360mg; Total Carbohydrates: 5g; Dietary Fiber: 2g; Sugars: Ig; Protein: 7g.

Using Rice Paper Wrappers

In place of lettuce leaves as wrappers for Asian-style veggie burger mixtures, try squares of rice paper, available in ethnic markets and the Asian foods section of well-stocked supermarkets. To prepare them, pour hot water into a shallow dish large enough to hold a wrapper flat. Soak until softened and pliable, about I5 seconds. Remove from the water and place on a flat work surface. Top with the filling—here, veggie burger strips sautéed with garlic, pepper flakes, and shredded carrots, plus thin strips of raw bell pepper and fresh mint leaves. Fold the sides of the rice paper over the filling, then roll up, pressing the edge to seal.

Tomato-Basil Burger Caprese Salad

To give this protein-rich main-course version of the popular tomato-and-mozzarella salad even more zest, look for veggie burgers with Italian-style seasonings. Widely available mixed baby salad greens (see sidebar) *speed assembly.*

Preparation Time: 20 minutes | Total Time: 20 minutes | Servings: 4

4 *Morningstar Farms*
Tomato & Basil Pizza Burgers

- or -

4 other *Morningstar Farms*
Veggie Burgers of your choice

4 cups mixed baby salad leaves or torn mixed greens

4 tablespoons bottled balsamic-basil vinaigrette salad dressing or balsamic vinaigrette salad dressing

4 small tomatoes, sliced

4 ounces fresh mozzarella cheese, sliced, or 1 cup shredded mozzarella cheese

8 teaspoons balsamic vinegar

½ teaspoon coarsely ground black pepper

For best results, see our tips on pages 8-9.

1. Cook burgers according to package directions.

2. Meanwhile, in mixing bowl, toss together salad leaves and salad dressing. Arrange in beds on serving plates or platter.

3. Top salad greens with tomatoes and burgers. Tuck cheese in between or arrange on top. Drizzle with vinegar. Sprinkle with pepper.

ON THE GRILL: Preheat the grill. Use a food thermometer to make sure patties reach minimum internal temperature of 160°F.

NUTRITION FACTS: Serving Size: 1 Salad; Calories: 310; Calories from Fat: 180; Total Fat: 20g; Saturated Fat: 7g; Cholesterol: 30mg; Sodium: 580mg; Total Carbohydrates: 17g; Dietary Fiber: 5g; Sugars: 9g; Protein: 17g.

Sorting Through Mixed Baby Salad Leaves

Once an item you might find only in fancy restaurants, mixed baby salad leaves are now available in many supermarkets, prewashed, sealed in plastic bags, and ready to use. When you buy them, check the "sell by" or "use by" date stamped on the packaging to make sure you're getting the freshest product. Before use, always quickly sort through the leaves *(below)* to remove any damaged or wilted items.

Spicy Asian Spinach Salad

Strips of veggie burger turn an Asian version of a classic wilted spinach salad (see sidebar) *into a delicious main course. Look for garlic chili sauce in the Asian foods section of your supermarket.*

Preparation Time: 25 minutes I Total Time: 25 minutes I Servings: 4

4 *Morningstar Farms*
Asian Veggie Patties

 - or -

4 other *Morningstar Farms*
Veggie Burgers of your choice

6½ cups loosely packed fresh
baby spinach (about 8 ounces)

½ cup sliced red bell pepper

2 tablespoons chopped
fresh cilantro

2 tablespoons chopped
fresh mint leaves

2 tablespoons vegetable oil

½ medium red onion, thinly sliced

2 cloves garlic, minced

1 teaspoon grated gingerroot

¼ cup cider vinegar

4 teaspoons reduced-sodium
soy sauce

1 tablespoon sugar

1 tablespoon garlic chili sauce

*For best results, see our tips
on pages 8-9.*

1. Cook burgers according to package directions.

2. Meanwhile, in large bowl, toss together spinach, bell pepper, cilantro, and mint. Set aside.

3. In 12-inch nonstick skillet, heat oil over medium heat. Add onion and cook, stirring frequently, until very tender, about 5 minutes. Stir in garlic and ginger. Cook and stir for 30 seconds. Carefully stir in vinegar, soy sauce, sugar, and chili sauce. Bring to boiling. Remove from heat. Add spinach mixture. Toss just until spinach begins to wilt.

4. Arrange spinach mixture on four serving plates. Cut veggie burgers into strips and arrange on top of salads. Serve immediately.

NUTRITION FACTS: Serving Size: I Salad; Calories: 200; Calories from Fat: 100; Total Fat: IIg; Saturated Fat: Ig; Cholesterol: 0mg; Sodium: 770mg; Total Carbohydrates: 16g; Dietary Fiber: 4g; Sugars: 6g; Protein: 9g.

Wilting a Spinach Salad

Most people know wilted spinach salads from long-popular versions featuring bacon and chopped egg. But even a healthier veggie burger version is basically made in the same way. First, prepare the spinach and other salad ingredients and set aside. Then, make the hot dressing in a skillet large enough for tossing the salad leaves. Finally, add the spinach mixture and toss quickly and briefly, using kitchen tongs *(right)*, just until the leaves are partially wilted but still have an edge of crispness.

Italian Herb *Chik Patties* Salad

Chinese chicken salad meets veggie burgers in this simple recipe featuring Morningstar Farms Chik Patties. *It's easy to vary the recipe to your own tastes* (see sidebar).

Preparation Time: 20 minutes | Total Time: 20 minutes | Servings: 2

2 *Morningstar Farms Chik Patties* Italian Herb

- or -

2 *Morningstar Farms Chik Patties* Parmesan Ranch

1 medium Portobello mushroom, sliced ¼ inch thick

½ small onion, sliced

4 teaspoons olive oil or vegetable oil

4 cloves garlic, minced

4 teaspoons reduced-sodium soy sauce

2 cups torn mixed spring greens or torn mixed greens

2 tablespoons Asian sesame with ginger salad dressing or balsamic vinaigrette salad dressing

2 tablespoons sliced almonds

2 teaspoons chopped fresh cilantro

For best results, see our tips on pages 8-9.

1. Cook patties according to package directions. Cut into slices ½ inch wide.

2. Meanwhile, in large nonstick skillet, cook mushroom and onion in hot oil, stirring frequently, until tender, about 3 minutes. Stir in garlic. Cook and stir for 30 seconds more. Carefully stir in soy sauce. Cook and stir until liquid evaporates, about 1 minute.

3. In mixing bowl, toss together greens and salad dressing. Arrange on serving plates. Top with mushroom mixture, patties, almonds, and cilantro.

NUTRITION FACTS: Serving Size: 1 Salad; Calories: 400; Calories from Fat: 220; Total Fat: 24g; Saturated Fat: 3g; Cholesterol: 0mg; Sodium: 490mg; Total Carbohydrates: 35g; Dietary Fiber: 6g; Sugars: 6g; Protein: 15g.

Honey-Sesame Asian Chik Patties *Salad*

Want to try a different style of Asian salad? In a medium mixing bowl, whisk together 1 tablespoon vegetable oil, ¼ cup vinegar, ¼ cup honey, 1 teaspoon soy sauce, 1 tablespoon sesame seeds, and ½ teaspoon toasted sesame oil. Cover and refrigerate. Prepare 4 *Morningstar Farms Chik Patties* of your choice according to package directions and cut into strips ½ inch wide. In large mixing bowl, toss together 4 cups bite-sized pieces rinsed and dried romaine lettuce, ½ cup sliced mushrooms, and 1 small tomato cut into wedges. Mound salad on individual serving plates and place strips of *Chik Patties* on top. Drizzle with dressing or pass dressing separately. Serves 4.

Chik Patties Italian Herb Fruit Salad

In this refreshing salad, the lively flavor of chicken-flavored veggie burger patties finds perfect complements in juicy fruit chunks and raspberry vinaigrette dressing. Prepackaged mixes of salad greens (page 46) make it even more convenient to prepare the recipe, which can easily be doubled or quadrupled.

Preparation Time: 20 minutes | Total Time: 20 minutes | Servings: 2

2 patties *Morningstar Farms Chik Patties* Italian Herb

- or -

2 patties *Morningstar Farms Chik Patties* Parmesan Ranch Breaded Veggie Patties

2 cups torn mixed spring greens, torn mixed greens, or mixed baby greens

2 tablespoons bottled raspberry poppy seed vinaigrette salad dressing or raspberry vinaigrette salad dressing

½ cup quartered fresh strawberries

¼ cup chopped fresh pineapple or canned pineapple, drained

¼ cup canned mandarin orange sections, drained

6 macadamia nuts or walnuts, toasted *(see sidebar, below)* and coarsely chopped

¼ teaspoon coarsely ground black pepper

For best results, see our tips on pages 8-9.

1. Cook patties according to package directions. Cut into slices ½ inch wide.

2. In small bowl, toss together greens and salad dressing. Arrange in individual mixing bowls or on serving plates. Top with strawberries, pineapple, orange sections, and nuts. Add patty slices. Sprinkle with pepper.

ON THE GRILL: Preheat the grill. Use a food thermometer to make sure patties reach minimum internal temperature of 160°F.

NUTRITION FACTS: Serving Size: 1 Salad; Calories: 330; Calories from Fat: 140; Total Fat: 15g; Saturated Fat: 2g; Trans Fat: 0g; Cholesterol: 0mg; Sodium: 130mg; Total Carbohydrates: 41g; Dietary Fiber: 6g; Sugars: 14g; Protein: 12g.

Toasting Nuts for Flavor and Texture

Nuts can add rich flavor and delightful crunch to many vegetarian dishes. Toasting nuts enhances both their taste and their texture. To toast a small quantity, put them in a small, dry skillet and cook over low heat, stirring frequently *(right)*, until they darken slightly in color and are fragrant. Immediately transfer to a bowl to cool. To toast a larger quantity, spread them evenly in a baking pan or on a baking sheet. Bake at 350°F until light golden brown, 5 to 10 minutes, stirring once or twice; then, transfer to a bowl or plate to cool. Whichever method you use, always take care not to overcook them. The nuts will continue to darken slightly after you remove them from the heat.

Summer Blue Burger Salad

When summer days and nights are hot, use the outdoor grill to cook veggie burgers and onions for this cool, refreshing salad. You'll like it so much you'll want to make it indoors, too, when the weather turns cool.

Preparation Time: 10 minutes | Total Time: 15 minutes | Servings: 4

3 tablespoons cider vinegar

3 tablespoons olive oil

½ teaspoon dried rosemary leaves

¼ teaspoon dried thyme leaves

¼ teaspoon salt

¼ teaspoon freshly ground black pepper

2 slices red onion, each about ¼ inch thick

4 *Morningstar Farms Grillers* Original Veggie Burgers

- or -

4 other *Morningstar Farms* Veggie Burgers of your choice

6 cups torn romaine lettuce

1 ounce crumbled blue cheese

2 tablespoons chopped walnuts, toasted *(see sidebar, page 53)*

For best results, see our tips on pages 8-9.

1. In jar with tight-fitting lid, combine vinegar, oil, rosemary, thyme, salt, and pepper. Cover and shake well.

2. Preheat outdoor or indoor grill, grill pan, or broiler.

3. Lightly brush onion on both sides with some vinegar mixture. Grill onion and frozen burgers over medium heat for 4 to 6 minutes, turning once, using a food thermometer to be sure patties reach minimum internal temperature of 160°F. Remove from grill.

4. Arrange lettuce on individual plates. Cut burgers into strips about ½ inch wide. Separate onion slices into rings. Arrange burger strips and onion rings on top of lettuce. Sprinkle with blue cheese and walnuts. Cover and shake remaining vinegar mixture. Drizzle over salads. Serve immediately.

NUTRITION FACTS: Serving Size: 1 Salad; Calories: 300; Calories from Fat: 190; Total Fat: 21g; Saturated Fat: 4.5g; Cholesterol: 5mg; Sodium: 510mg; Total Carbohydrates: 10g; Dietary Fiber: 5g; Sugars: 3g; Protein: 18g.

Chilling Romaine Leaves

Part of the pleasure of the salad recipe on this page, and others featuring romaine lettuce, is the contrast between the warm veggie burgers and the cool, crisp leaves. To accentuate the texture of these crunchy salad leaves, after rinsing them, arrange the leaves in a single layer on a length of heavy-duty paper towels or a clean kitchen towel. Roll up *(right)* and put the bundle in the refrigerator to chill the leaves for an hour or more before unrolling them and tearing into bite-sized pieces.

Spicy Black Bean Burger Tex-Mex Salad

Whenever you crave a spicy, satisfying main-dish salad, everything you need is ready and waiting at most supermarkets—or possibly even in your own well-stocked kitchen. This recipe is so simple to prepare that you can easily double or quadruple it to feed family or friends.

Preparation Time: 20 minutes | Total Time: 20 minutes | Servings: 1

1 *Morningstar Farms* Spicy Black Bean Veggie Burger

- *or* -

1 other *Morningstar Farms* Veggie Burger of your choice

1 cup torn mixed spring greens or torn mixed greens

1 tablespoon bottled sun-dried tomato vinaigrette salad dressing or spicy ranch salad dressing

3 grape tomatoes or cherry tomatoes, halved

2 tablespoons shredded Cheddar cheese with jalapeño peppers or Monterey Jack cheese with jalapeño peppers

1 tablespoon prepared tomato salsa

1 tablespoon prepared guacamole

1 tablespoon fat-free sour cream

For best results, see our tips on pages 8-9.

1. Cook veggie burger according to package directions. Cut into bite-sized pieces.

2. Meanwhile, in small bowl, toss together greens and salad dressing. Arrange on serving plate. Top with tomatoes and cheese. Arrange burger pieces on top. Spoon salsa, guacamole, and sour cream over burger.

NUTRITION FACTS: Serving Size: I Salad; Calories: 290; Calories from Fat: I30; Total Fat: I4g; Saturated Fat: 4g; Cholesterol: I5mg; Sodium: 790mg; Total Carbohydrates: 26g; Dietary Fiber: 7g; Sugars: 6g; Protein: I7g.

Making a Stacked Tostada Salad

If you have just a little extra time and want to impress your guests with spectacular tostada salads, look for I2 packaged crispy round corn tortillas made especially for tostadas. Mash I ripe pitted and peeled avocado with ½ cup spicy ranch salad dressing and I tablespoon lime juice. Cook 4 of your favorite spicy veggie burgers in a large nonstick skillet according to package directions, then cool slightly and cut into strips. In the same skillet, sauté I cup thawed frozen corn kernels until beginning to brown, I to 3 minutes. In large bowl, toss together burger strips, corn, 4 cups torn romaine lettuce, I large chopped plum tomato, ½ cup each shredded cheddar and Monterey Jack with peppers, and another ripe avocado, chopped. Spread salad dressing mixture over I side of each crispy corn tortilla. For each salad, place a tortilla, dressing side up, on each of 4 serving plates. Top with some lettuce mixture, a second tortilla, more lettuce mixture; a third tortilla; and more lettuce mixture. Garnish with salsa, sour cream, and onions.

Fire and Ice Pasta Salad

Bite-sized pasta tubes provide the perfect backdrop for this healthful salad's bright flavors of hot chili pepper, cool tropical fruit, and spicy veggie burgers

Preparation Time: 20 minutes I Total Time: 2 hours 20 minutes I Servings: 4

4 ounces dried penne pasta or other bite-sized pasta tubes or shapes of your choice *(see sidebar)*

2 *Morningstar Farms* Tex Mex Burgers made with Organic Soy

- or -

2 other *Morningstar Farms* Veggie Burgers of your choice

2 medium mangoes, peeled, seeded, and coarsely chopped

1 medium tomato, seeded and coarsely chopped

1 medium jalapeño pepper, seeded and finely chopped

⅓ cup picante salsa

2 tablespoons lime juice

1 tablespoon honey

1 teaspoon olive oil

Lettuce leaves, for serving

For best results, see our tips on pages 8-9.

1. Cook pasta according to package directions. Drain. Rinse with cold water. Drain and transfer to large mixing bowl.

2. Cook burgers according to package directions. Cut each patty into 9 pieces. Add to pasta along with mangoes, tomato, and jalapeño pepper. Gently but thoroughly toss. Cover with plastic wrap and refrigerate for 2 hours.

3. In small bowl, whisk together picante salsa, lime juice, honey, and oil. Drizzle over chilled salad. Lightly toss to coat.

4. To serve, line 4 salad plates or bowls with lettuce leaves. Mound salad in center.

NUTRITION FACTS: Serving Size: I Salad, about 2 cups; Calories: 270; Calories from Fat: 30; Total Fat: 3g; Saturated Fat: 0g; Cholesterol: 0mg; Sodium: 480mg; Total Carbohydrates: 56g; Dietary Fiber: 5g; Sugars: 26g; Protein: I0g.

Veggie Burger Pasta Salads

With its mild, earthy flavor and chewy texture, pasta is like a blank canvas on which you can create all sorts of edible artworks by adding your favorite veggie burgers, dressings, and other ingredients. For an Asian Pasta Salad *(right)* that serves 8, cook and drain 16 ounces bow tie pasta. Toss with 8 ounces blanched snow pea pods, I diced red bell pepper, ½ cup diced celery, and ½ cup chopped green onion. Add a dressing of 3 tablespoons Dijon mustard, 2 tablespoons vinegar, I tablespoon toasted sesame oil, 2 teaspoons sugar, ½ teaspoon soy sauce, the juice squeezed from a grated peeled 4-inch piece fresh ginger, and I tablespoon toasted sesame seeds. Toss again and chill. Before serving, prepare 4 veggie burgers according to package directions and cut into strips ¼ inch thick. Toss with pasta mixture and serve.

Minestrone Casserole

Chunks of flavorful veggie burger turn this easy version of the classic Italian minestrone into a hearty starter or main course packed with pasta and beans. Veggie burgers make great additions to casseroles, whether simmered on the stovetop as in this recipe or baked in the oven (see sidebar).

Preparation Time: 20 minutes | Total Time: 40 minutes | Servings: 8

4 *Morningstar Farms*
Tomato & Basil Pizza Burgers

- or -

4 other *Morningstar Farms*
Veggie Burgers of your choice

3 cups cooked small shell
or rotelle pasta

1 package (16 ounces) frozen
mixed vegetables

1 can (14.5 ounces) cannellini
or kidney beans

1 can (14.5 ounces) diced tomatoes

1 teaspoon minced garlic

1 teaspoon salt

¼ teaspoon black pepper

2 teaspoons Italian seasoning

½ cup freshly grated
Parmesan cheese

*For best results, see our tips
on pages 8-9.*

1. Cut veggie burgers into bite-sized pieces. Place in large saucepan. Add cooked pasta, mixed vegetables, beans, tomatoes, garlic, salt, pepper, and Italian seasoning.

2. Cook over medium heat, stirring occasionally, until mixture begins to boil. Reduce heat, cover, and simmer until thoroughly heated and thickened, about 15 minutes.

3. Ladle minestrone casserole into large individual serving bowls. Serve hot, garnished with Parmesan cheese.

NUTRITION FACTS: Serving Size: 1 cup; Calories: 250; Calories from Fat: 45; Total Fat: 5g; Saturated Fat: 0.5g; Cholesterol: 0mg; Sodium: 570mg; Total Carbohydrates: 35g; Dietary Fiber: 10g; Sugars: 5g; Protein: 19g.

An Easy Main-Dish Veggie Casserole

Combined in one dish with cooked pasta or rice, fresh, frozen, or canned vegetables, seasonings, and maybe some cheese, veggie burgers make easy, complete, and satisfying casserole meals. For a California Zucchini Bake *(right)*, heat 1 tablespoon vegetable oil in large skillet and sauté chunks of 4 veggie burgers with 3 cups sliced zucchini and ½ cup chopped onion until heated through. Remove from heat and stir in 1 teaspoon chili powder, ½ teaspoon each salt and garlic powder, 1 can (4½ ounces) chopped roasted green chilies, 2 cups cooked rice or small cooked pasta, ½ cup reduced-fat sour cream, and ½ cup shredded Monterey Jack cheese. Place in shallow 2½-quart baking dish coated with vegetable cooking spray. Top with 1 large thinly sliced tomato and ½ cup more shredded cheese. Bake in preheated 375°F oven until heated through, about 20 minutes. Serve immediately. Serves 8.

Mini Pasta Frittatas

Frittatas, the rustic flat omelets of Italy, are often packed with chunks of vegetable or even pieces of pasta, and chunks of veggie burger make perfect additions. Baking the frittatas in the oven in muffin cups couldn't be easier, producing attractive treats to serve for a casual weeknight supper or weekend lunch or brunch.

Preparation Time: 25 minutes | Total Time: 50 minutes | Servings: 8

4 *Morningstar Farms*
Tomato & Basil Pizza Burgers

- or -

4 other *Morningstar Farms*
Veggie Burgers of your choice

8 large eggs, lightly beaten

4 ounces reduced-fat cream
cheese, softened

½ cup freshly grated
Parmesan cheese

½ cup milk

2 teaspoons dried oregano leaves

¼ teaspoon salt

¼ teaspoon black pepper

2 cups cooked spaghetti or other
pasta strands *(see sidebar)*

½ cup finely chopped
red bell pepper

2 cups prepared bottled
marinara sauce, warmed

*For best results, see our tips
on pages 8-9.*

1. Cut veggie burgers into bite-sized pieces. Set aside.

2. In large mixing bowl, beat together eggs, cream cheese, and Parmesan cheese. Stir in milk, oregano, salt, and pepper. Add burger pieces, spaghetti, and bell pepper. Stir until thoroughly combined.

3. Preheat oven to 350°F. Coat 8 large muffin-pan cups with vegetable cooking spray. Portion pasta mixture evenly into muffin cups.

4. Bake until frittatas are set and tops are browned, about 25 minutes. Carefully remove hot frittatas from muffin cups. Serve warm with marinara sauce.

NUTRITION FACTS: Serving Size: I Frittata; Calories: 310; Calories from Fat: 130; Total Fat: 14g; Saturated Fat: 6g; Cholesterol: 230mg; Sodium: 580mg; Total Carbohydrates: 24g; Dietary Fiber: 4g; Sugars: 8g; Protein: 20g.

Selecting Pasta Strands

Most supermarkets today offer a wide variety of good-quality dried pastas from different manufacturers. In addition to the stringlike spaghetti called for in the recipe above *(shown second from the right in the photo)*, other options include *(from far right)* thin angel hair; perciatelli, resembling thick, hollow spaghetti; narrow linguini ribbons; and slightly wider tagliatelli. Regardless of the pasta you use, always cook it what Italians call *al dente*, tender but still chewy, following suggested cooking times on the package.

Bow Tie Lasagna

When you want all the hearty flavor of great lasagna without all the work of preparing a sauce and layering and baking the pasta and other ingredients, try this simple slow-cooker recipe.

Preparation Time: 30 minutes | Total Time: 3 hours 30 minutes | Servings: 6

3¾ cups (8 ounces) uncooked bow tie pasta

4 *Morningstar Farms* Tomato & Basil Pizza Burgers

- or -

4 other *Morningstar Farms* Veggie Burgers of your choice

2 cups (8 ounces) shredded mozzarella cheese

16 ounces low-fat cottage cheese

1 jar (26 ounces) fat-free spaghetti sauce

1 cup water

¼ teaspoon salt

¼ teaspoon pepper

1 teaspoon Italian seasoning blend

2 tablespoons dried parsley flakes

For best results, see our tips on pages 8-9.

1. Cook pasta according to package directions. Drain and spread evenly in bottom of slow cooker.

2. Cut veggie burgers into bite-sized pieces and arrange in even layer on top of pasta in slow cooker *(see sidebar)*. Spread mozzarella and cottage cheese on top of veggie burgers, and then evenly pour in spaghetti sauce and water and sprinkle evenly with salt, pepper, and Italian seasoning. Stir lightly to combine.

3. Place lid securely on slow cooker, set to low-heat setting, and cook until thoroughly heated through and bubbly, about 3 hours. Stir in parsley and serve immediately.

NUTRITION FACTS: Serving Size: 1⅓ cups; Calories: 380; Calories from Fat: 110; Total Fat: 12g; Saturated Fat: 6g; Cholesterol: 30mg; Sodium: 1200mg; Total Carbohydrates: 36g; Dietary Fiber: 5g; Sugars: 12g; Protein: 32g.

Using a Slow Cooker

Modern slow cookers come in a range of sizes, from small ones measuring 1½ to 2½ quarts to large ones holding 5 to 7 quarts, and in round or oval shapes. They consist of a glazed stoneware crock placed securely inside an electrically controlled casing that heats the crock. All offer the option of low-heat and high-heat settings, and most include timers as well. When putting food in a slow cooker, always distribute it as evenly as possible *(right)* so that it heats through and cooks evenly at the relatively low cooking temperatures.

Vegan Veggie Burger Lasagna Rolls

Try this unusual, easy-to-serve way to prepare lasagna by rolling up individual lasagna noodles around the filling.

Preparation Time: 25 minutes | Total Time: 1 hour 15 minutes | Servings: 4

8 dried lasagna noodles

6 ounces firm tofu, drained

1 tablespoon lemon juice

1 tablespoon soy milk

2 cloves garlic, minced

3 tablespoons chopped fresh basil

1 package (10 ounces) frozen chopped spinach, thawed in microwave for 30 seconds

2 cups bottled vegan marinara sauce

4 *Morningstar Farms Grillers* Vegan Veggie Burgers, cut into strips

For best results, see our tips on pages 8-9.

1. Cook noodles according to package directions. Drain. Rinse with cold water. Drain again. Pat dry with paper towels.

2. While noodles are cooking, in food processor fitted with stainless-steel blade combine tofu, lemon juice, soy milk, and garlic. Cover and process until nearly smooth. Transfer to mixing bowl and stir in basil. Set aside.

3. Drain spinach in colander, pressing with back of spoon to remove excess moisture.

4. Preheat oven to 350°F.

5. Meanwhile, in 11-by-7-by-2-inch baking dish, spread 1 cup of the marinara sauce. On work surface, spread tofu mixture on one side of each lasagna noodle. Top with veggie burger strips. Sprinkle with spinach. Roll up each noodle. Place rolls, seam side down, on top of sauce in baking dish. Spoon remaining sauce on top.

6. Cover dish tightly with foil. Bake in preheated oven for 40 minutes. Remove foil. Let stand for 10 minutes before serving.

NUTRITION FACTS: Serving Size: 2 Lasagna Rolls; Calories: 410; Calories from Fat: 90; Total Fat: 10g; Saturated Fat: 1.5g; Cholesterol: 0mg; Sodium: 930mg; Total Carbohydrates: 53g; Dietary Fiber: 11g; Sugars: 9g; Protein: 27g.

A Traditional Layered Lasagna

For a layered lasagna that serves 6, combine in a mixing bowl 1 can (14½ ounces) diced Italian-style tomatoes, 1 jar (14 ounces) spaghetti sauce, 1 package *Morningstar Farms* Veggie Burgers cut into small chunks. Spread ⅓ of mixture in the bottom of an 11-by-7-inch baking dish. Arrange ½ an 8-ounce package of uncooked lasagna noodles on top. Spread ½ of a 16-ounce carton fat-free cottage cheese on top. Top with another ⅓ of tomato mixture, then remaining noodles, cottage cheese, and remaining sauce. Cover with foil and bake in a preheated 350°F oven for 50 minutes. Uncover, sprinkle with ¾ cup shredded mozzarella cheese and 2 tablespoons grated Parmesan cheese and bake, uncovered, until cheese melts, about 5 minutes. Let stand for 10 minutes, sprinkle with 2 tablespoons chopped parsley, and serve, cut into squares.

Chik Patties Parmesan

Bake a chicken-flavored veggie patty you love with a topping of tomato sauce and cheese on top of a bed of bite-sized pasta shapes and you have a great new version of an old Italian trattoria standby, often called "Parmesan" or alla Parmigiana, even if featuring another kind of cheese.

Preparation Time: 40 minutes | Total Time: 50 minutes | Servings: 4

½ cup chopped onion

2 cloves minced garlic

1 tablespoon olive oil

12 ounces tomato paste

2½ cups water

1¼ teaspoons dried oregano

1¼ teaspoons dried basil

1 teaspoon sugar

⅛ teaspoon pepper

4 *Morningstar Farms Chik Patties* Original

- or -

4 other *Morningstar Farms Chik Patties* of your choice

- or -

4 other *Morningstar Farms* Veggie Burgers of your choice

2 cups cooked pasta

4 ounces shredded low-fat Mozzarella cheese

2 tablespoons dried parsley flakes

For best results, see our tips on pages 8-9.

1. In large saucepan, sauté onion and garlic in oil over medium heat, stirring frequently, until tender. Add tomato paste, water, oregano, basil, sugar, and pepper. Heat until boiling, stirring frequently. Reduce heat and simmer 30 minutes, stirring occasionally.

2. Preheat oven to 350°F. Prepare veggie patties according to package directions.

3. Pour cooked pasta into 2-quart baking dish coated with vegetable cooking spray. Spoon I cup sauce evenly over pasta. Neatly arrange veggie patties on top of pasta and sprinkle evenly with ½ of the cheese. Spoon remaining sauce on top of patties and sprinkle with remaining cheese and parsley flakes. Bake until thoroughly heated through and cheese is melted, I0 to I5 minutes.

4. With large serving spoon, scoop hot veggie patties and pasta onto individual serving plates. Serve immediately.

NUTRITION FACTS: Serving Size: I Patty plus about ½ cup pasta and sauce; Calories: 480; Calories from Fat: I65; Total Fat: I8g; Saturated Fat: 5.25g; Cholesterol: I5mg; Sodium: 735mg; Total Carbohydrates: 54g; Dietary Fiber: 7.5g; Sugars: I3.5g; Protein: 24g.

New Twists on an Italian Favorite

Want to make the above recipe your own? It's easy. Substitute cooked whole-wheat or regular pasta strands *(see sidebar, page 62)* for bite-sized shapes and, while cooking the pasta, add fresh seasonal vegetables such as broccoli florets, baby carrots, and red bell pepper strips to the boiling water for the last 3 minutes. If you like, use bottled prepared marinara sauce instead of making it yourself. Prepare *Morningstar Farms Chik Patties* Breaded Veggie Patties according to package directions. Either assemble and bake the dish as described above or, instead, simply place hot veggie patties on top of drained pasta-vegetable mixture, spoon warmed sauce on top, and garnish with shredded cheese.

Szechwan Noodle Stir-Fry

A wok or large skillet makes it incredibly easy to stir up these colorful, delicious, lightly spicy Chinese-style noodles with chunks of veggie burger. But don't limit your stir-fried noodles to Asian flavors alone (see sidebar)*!*

Preparation Time: 30 minutes | Total Time: 30 minutes | Servings: 6

4 *Morningstar Farms*
Asian Veggie Patties

- or -

4 other *Morningstar Farms*
Veggie Burgers of your choice

¼ cup reduced-sodium soy sauce

2 tablespoons rice vinegar

¼ to ½ teaspoon crushed
red pepper flakes

¼ teaspoon ground ginger

1 package (9 ounces) refrigerated
fresh egg linguine or fresh Chinese
egg noodles

1 tablespoon vegetable oil

1 medium onion, cut into
thin slivers (about 1½ cups)

2 cloves garlic, minced

2 cups baby carrots,
quartered lengthwise

2 cups broccoli florets

*For best results, see our tips
on pages 8-9.*

1. Cook veggie burgers according to package directions. Cut each patty into 8 wedges. Set aside. Keep warm.

2. Meanwhile, in small bowl, stir together soy sauce, vinegar, red pepper flakes, and ginger. Set aside.

3. Cook noodles according to package directions, omitting any salt or oil. Drain. Rinse with cold water. Drain well. Set aside.

4. Put oil in large nonstick wok or 12-inch skillet. Preheat over high heat. Add onion and garlic and stir-fry for 3 to 4 minutes or until tender. Add carrots. Stir-fry for 2 minutes more. Add broccoli. Stir-fry until all vegetables are tender-crisp, 1 to 3 minutes longer. Add pasta, veggie burger wedges, and soy sauce mixture. Stir until heated through and all ingredients are evenly coated with sauce.

5. Transfer noodle mixture to individual serving plates or bowls. Serve immediately.

NUTRITION FACTS: Serving Size: about 7 ounces; Calories: 300; Calories from Fat: 70; Total Fat: 8g; Saturated Fat: 1.5g; Cholesterol: 85mg; Sodium: 770mg; Total Carbohydrates: 46g; Dietary Fiber: 4g; Sugars: 8g; Protein: 13g.

Putting a Mediterranean Spin on Stir-fried Pasta

The same quick stir-frying or sautéing that produces a fragrant veggie burger noodle recipe like the one above can also be adapted to the seasonings and styles of other cuisines. For a quick Sicilian-style veggie burger pasta dish that serves 1, cook a veggie burger according to package directions and cut into bite-sized pieces. In a nonstick saucepan or wok, cook 2 cloves garlic, minced, in 2 teaspoons hot olive oil for 30 seconds. Then, stir in 2 tablespoons drained and chopped oil-packed sun-dried tomatoes, 1 tablespoon sliced pitted black olives, and 1 tablespoon sliced almonds; sauté or stir-fry over medium heat until almonds begin to brown, 2 to 3 minutes. Carefully add ¼ cup reduced-sodium vegetable broth or dry white wine and gently boil until most of liquid evaporates. Toss with 1 cup hot cooked small penne or other bite-sized pasta, top with veggie burger pieces and 1 teaspoon chopped fresh parsley, and serve immediately.

Italian Porcupine Balls

Serve these savory home-style Mediterranean bundles on their own, passing the sauce on the side. Or try making smaller ones and serving them along with the sauce on top of your favorite pasta.

Preparation Time: 25 minutes | Total Time: 40 minutes | Servings: 4

4 *Morningstar Farms* Tomato & Basil Pizza Burgers

- *or* -

4 other *Morningstar Farms* Veggie Burgers of your choice

1 large egg, slightly beaten

1 can (10¾ ounces) condensed tomato soup

½ cup finely chopped onion

1 cup cooked rice

1 tablespoon dried parsley flakes

½ cup water

1 tablespoon Worcestershire sauce

For best results, see our tips on pages 8-9.

1. Cut veggie burgers into small pieces. Set aside.

2. In medium-sized mixing bowl, combine egg and ¼ cup of the tomato soup. Add veggie burger pieces, onion, rice, and parsley. Stir until thoroughly combined.

3. With clean hands lightly moistened with water, portion and shape mixture into 8 equal balls. Place in large frying pan.

4. In small bowl, stir together remainder of soup, water, and Worcestershire sauce. Pour over balls. Cook over medium heat until mixture begins to boil. Reduce heat, cover, and continue cooking for 15 minutes. Serve hot.

NUTRITION FACTS: Serving Size: 2 Porcupine Balls; Calories: 275; Calories from Fat: 90; Total Fat: 10g; Saturated Fat: 1.5g; Cholesterol: 55mg; Sodium: 510mg; Total Carbohydrates: 22g; Dietary Fiber: 3g; Sugars: 3g; Protein: 19g.

Making Veggie Burger Meatballs

As the recipe above demonstrates, it's incredibly easy to transform your favorite veggie burgers into delicious meatballs. For an even easier twist that yields 32 bite-sized barbecue-flavored meatballs *(right)* perfect to pass as a party appetizer or hors d'oeuvre, defrost 4 *Morningstar Farms Grillers* Vegan Veggie Burgers or other favorite variety of *Morningstar Farms* Veggie Burgers overnight in the refrigerator or for 1 hour at room temperature.

With clean hands, divide and shape each burger into 8 round balls, rolling them between your palms. Place on an ungreased baking sheet and bake in a preheated 350°F oven for 15 minutes. Meanwhile, combine 1 bottle (18 ounces) barbecue sauce and 2 tablespoons lemon juice in a medium-sized saucepan and cook over low heat until hot. Place the baked balls in the warm sauce. For serving at a party, transfer to a chafing dish or a slow cooker on the low-heat setting.

Spicy Black Bean Dip

Try preparing this wonderfully flavorful hot dip recipe for your next party. A slow cooker (see sidebar, page 65) *makes it so easy to put together, though you can also prepare it and other thick dips on the stovetop* (see sidebar). *Serve with baked tortilla chips or fresh vegetables such as celery sticks, for dipping.*

Preparation Time: 10 minutes | Total Time: 3 hours 10 minutes | Servings: 10

4 *Morningstar Farms*
Spicy Black Bean Veggie Burgers

1 package (16 ounces) light processed cheese product, cubed

1 package (8 ounces) Neufchatel cheese, cubed

1 jar (16 ounces) medium-spicy thick-and-chunky salsa

½ cup water

2 tablespoons chopped fresh cilantro

For best results, see our tips on pages 8-9.

1. Cut up veggie burgers into small pieces and distribute evenly in a slow cooker. Evenly scatter in cubed cheeses, spoon in salsa, and pour in water. Stir lightly to combine.

2. Cover slow cooker and cook on low-heat setting until mixture is hot, thick, and bubbly, about 3 hours, very briefly uncovering and stirring it occasionally.

3. Stir in cilantro and serve from slow cooker or in serving bowls.

NUTRITION FACTS: Serving Size: ½ cup; Calories: 230; Calories from Fat: 100; Total Fat: 12g; Saturated Fat: 7g; Cholesterol: 30mg; Sodium: 1180mg; Total Carbohydrates: 15g; Dietary Fiber: 2g; Sugars: 8g; Protein: 17g.

Stirring Up a Batch of Tex-Mex Bean Dip

To stir up a quick veggie burger dip on the stovetop, first transfer a 15½-ounce can of chili beans to a mixing bowl and partially mash with a wooden spoon. Set aside. In a 12-inch skillet over medium heat, sauté ½ cup chopped onion in 1 tablespoon vegetable oil until soft and fragrant. Add 4 *Morningstar Farms Grillers* Vegan Veggie Burgers or other favorite *Morningstar Farms* Veggie Burgers and continue cooking over medium heat, stirring frequently with a wooden spoon and breaking up the burgers into small pieces, for 2 minutes. Stir in beans, ½ cup diced tomatoes, ½ cup thick-and-chunky salsa, ½ cup shredded low-fat mozzarella cheese, ¼ cup chopped fresh cilantro, 1 tablespoon lime juice, and ¼ teaspoon garlic powder. Continue cooking, stirring frequently, until cheese melts completely and mixture is hot. Serve immediately.

Barley Vegetable Soup

Start this recipe in the slow cooker when you begin your day, then come home in the evening to some of the most heartwarming soup imaginable. Adding veggie burgers yields a meal that is nutritious and full of flavor.

Preparation Time: 20 minutes | Total Time: 8 hours 20 minutes | Servings: 8

4 *Morningstar Farms Grillers Prime* Veggie Burgers

- or -

4 other *Morningstar Farms* Veggie Burgers of your choice

1 package (16 ounces) frozen mixed vegetables

1 cup chopped celery

½ cup chopped onion

1 can (28 ounces) diced tomatoes

½ cup pearl barley

2 extra-large vegetarian vegetable bouillon cubes

5 cups hot water

½ teaspoon salt

¼ teaspoon black pepper

For best results, see our tips on pages 8-9.

1. Cut veggie burgers into cubes and distribute evenly in bottom of slow cooker. Evenly scatter in mixed vegetables, celery, onion, tomatoes, and barley.

2. In large bowl, dissolve bouillon cubes in hot water. Pour over vegetables and veggie burgers. Season with salt and pepper.

3. Securely cover slow cooker and cook on low-heat setting until vegetables are tender, about 8 hours. To serve, ladle into soup bowls.

NUTRITION FACTS: Serving Size: 1½ cups; Calories: 190; Calories from Fat: 50; Total Fat: 5g; Saturated Fat: 1g; Cholesterol: 0mg; Sodium: 940mg; Total Carbohydrates: 26g; Dietary Fiber: 7g; Sugars: 5g; Protein: 12g.

Simmering a Pot of Tortilla Soup

Try enhancing other favorite soup recipes with veggie burgers. For a version of popular tortilla soup to serve 10 for a party, in a large saucepan, sauté 1 medium Spanish onion cut into ¼-inch dice, 1 each medium red and green bell peppers cut into ¼-inch dice, and 2 tablespoons minced garlic in 2 tablespoons canola oil over medium heat for 4 minutes. Stir in 2 quarts vegetable broth, 16 ounces canned stewed tomatoes, 10 ounces corn kernels, and 2 tablespoons chopped fresh cilantro. Bring to a boil, then reduce heat and simmer for 10 minutes, stirring occasionally. Stir in 5 *Morningstar Farms* Spicy Black Bean Veggie Burgers cut into ¼-inch dice and ¼ cup pureed canned chipotle pepper; continue simmering 6 to 8 minutes longer. Ladle into serving bowls, garnish with sour cream and Cheez-It® crackers, and pass fresh lime wedges.

Spicy Black Bean Chili

Spicy veggie burgers, especially those made with black beans, provide the ideal foundation for making a quick pan of hearty authentic-tasting Southwestern-style chili.

Preparation Time: 15 minutes | Total Time: 30 minutes | Servings: 6

1 tablespoon olive oil

1 cup chopped onion

1 teaspoon chopped garlic

2 tablespoons finely chopped fresh jalapeño peppers

8 *Morningstar Farms* Spicy Black Bean Veggie Burgers

2 cans (28 ounces each) crushed tomatoes

1 can (14.5 ounces) vegetable broth

2 cans (4.5 ounces each) chopped green chilies

2 tablespoons chipotle pepper sauce

Reduced-fat sour cream, for garnish

Reduced-fat shredded cheddar cheese, for garnish (optional)

For best results, see our tips on pages 8-9.

1. In large saucepan, heat oil over medium heat. Add onion, garlic, and jalapeño peppers and sauté, stirring occasionally, until fragrant and onion starts to turn translucent, 3 to 5 minutes.

2. Add veggie burgers and continue cooking, breaking up burgers into small pieces *(see sidebar)*. Continue until completely broken up and heated through.

3. Add tomatoes, vegetable broth, canned chilies, and pepper sauce and stir thoroughly. Cook until chili is completely heated through and thick, stirring occasionally, about 15 minutes.

4. Ladle into serving bowls. Pass sour cream and, if you like, cheese.

NUTRITION FACTS: Serving Size: 1¼ cups; Calories: 280; Calories from Fat: 40; Total Fat: 4.5g; Saturated Fat: 0.5g; Cholesterol: 5mg; Sodium: 1590mg; Total Carbohydrates: 42g; Dietary Fiber: 6g; Sugars: 11g; Protein: 20g.

Creating Your Own Veggie Burger Chili

It's a simple process to turn veggie burgers into the base for a bowlful of hearty chili. Start by sautéing any aromatic vegetables you like, including onions, garlic, and peppers. Then, add your veggie burgers of choice and continue sautéing, breaking up the burgers with the edge of a sturdy wooden spoon or spatula *(right)*. Depending on your tastes and the kind of veggie burgers you're using, add canned tomatoes or beans and such seasonings as chili powder, cumin, oregano, as well as a little salt and pepper to taste. Simmer until thick, adjust the heat level with your favorite hot sauce, add sour cream or shredded cheese, and you're ready to enjoy a satisfying treat.

Cheesy Black Bean Quesadilla Triangles

Most people think of quesadillas as simply tortillas folded over cheese and fried or broiled until crispy. This version, however, features a generous veggie burger filling and is baked in the oven until crispy.

Preparation Time: 25 minutes | Total Time: 35 minutes | Servings: 5

2 *Morningstar Farms*
Spicy Black Bean Veggie Burgers

½ cup prepared tomato salsa

½ cup shredded cheddar cheese or
Monterey Jack cheese (2 ounces)

¼ cup shredded pepper Jack
cheese (1 ounce)

2 teaspoons salt-free Southwest
or Mexican seasoning

10 (8-inch) flour tortillas

1 tablespoon unsalted butter
or margarine, melted

2½ cups shredded lettuce
(optional)

2 tablespoons finely chopped
red or green bell pepper

*For best results, see our tips
on pages 8-9.*

1. Thaw veggie burgers in microwave for 30 seconds. With clean hands, crumble into medium mixing bowl. Add salsa, cheeses, and seasoning. Stir until thoroughly combined.

2. Preheat oven to 375°F.

3. To shape and fill quesadillas *(see sidebar)*, use pizza cutter to trim tortillas into triangles with equal sides of about 7 inches. (Save trimmed edges for another use.) Place about 2 tablespoons veggie burger mixture in center of each triangle. One at a time, fold corners of triangle over filling, completely enclosing filling to make a small triangle-shaped parcel. Secure with toothpicks. Place on baking sheet, toothpick side up. Brush tops with butter or margarine.

4. Bake quesadillas until tops start to turn brown, 9 to 12 minutes. Arrange on top of shredded lettuce, if you like. Sprinkle with bell pepper. Serve immediately.

NUTRITION FACTS: Serving Size: 2 Triangles; Calories: 480; Calories from Fat: 150; Total Fat: 17g; Saturated Fat: 6g; Trans Fat: 1g; Cholesterol: 25mg; Sodium: 1030mg; Total Carbohydrates: 63g; Dietary Fiber: 6g; Sugars: 3g; Protein: 18g.

Shaping Quesadilla Triangles

The quesadilla triangles in this recipe can be filled with any combination you like of veggie burgers, cheeses, and seasonings. To shape them, start with 8-inch flour tortillas. Gently fold in the edges from 3 equally spaced spots on a tortilla's perimeter and, with a knife tip or pizza cutter, mark the spots along the edge where the creases meet. Then, place the tortilla flat on a work surface and, with a pizza cutter or sharp knife, neatly cut from 1 mark to the next to create 3 equal sides of a triangle. Place the filling in the center, then fold in the triangle's tips to overlap on top of the filling, which will still show at the corners. Push a wooden toothpick down through the overlapping tortilla tips *(right)* and into the filling.

Tex-Mex Enchiladas

The Southwestern favorite gets a vegan spin. If you prefer, use another kind of veggie burger and regular cheese.

Preparation Time: 30 minutes | Total Time: 50 minutes | Servings: 4

1½ cups tomato salsa

¾ cup chopped fresh cilantro

1 can (10 ounces)
red enchilada sauce

1 teaspoon ground cumin

2 *Morningstar Farms Grillers*
Vegan Veggie Burgers

- or -

2 other *Morningstar Farms*
Veggie Burgers of your choice

2 teaspoons vegetable oil

⅓ cup finely chopped red onion

¾ cup canned black beans,
rinsed and drained

8 (6-inch) corn tortillas

1½ cups shredded cheddar-flavored
soy cheese or cheddar cheese

2 cups shredded lettuce

*For best results, see our tips
on pages 8-9.*

1. In food processor fitted with stainless-steel blade, combine salsa and ½ cup of cilantro. Process until smooth. Transfer to bowl and set aside.

2. In shallow dish, stir together enchilada sauce, ¼ cup cilantro, and cumin. Set aside.

3. Thaw veggie burgers in microwave for 30 seconds. Heat oil in large nonstick skillet over medium heat. Add veggie burgers and onion and cook until burgers are heated through and onion is tender, stirring frequently and breaking up burgers into small pieces *(see sidebar, page 78)*, 2 to 3 minutes. Remove from heat. Stir in beans.

4. Preheat oven to 350°F.

5. In 11-by-7-by-2–inch baking dish, spread ⅓ cup enchilada sauce mixture. Dip tortillas, 1 at a time, in remaining enchilada sauce. Spoon burger mixture in center of tortillas. Roll up. Place, seam side down, on top of enchilada sauce in baking dish. Pour any remaining sauce over tortillas.

6. Cover baking dish tightly with aluminum foil. Bake in preheated oven for 15 minutes. Remove foil. Sprinkle with cheese. Continue baking until cheese has melted and enchiladas are heated through, 5 to 10 minutes. Serve with shredded lettuce and salsa mixture.

NUTRITION FACTS: Serving Size: 2 Enchiladas; Calories: 430; Calories from Fat: 90; Total Fat: 10g; Saturated Fat: 0g; Cholesterol: 0mg; Sodium: 2060mg; Total Carbohydrates: 56g; Dietary Fiber: 12g; Sugars: 5g; Protein: 25g.

Veggie Burger Enchilada Variations

Try other veggie burgers you like, as the basis for getting creative with enchilada fillings like the one in the recipe above. Try adding chopped tomato or canned mild green chilies to the filling and, if you aren't vegan, spread some fat-free sour cream on top. Most packaged corn tortillas are a little stiff and can split if you try to roll them up before softening them. In the recipe above, they are softened by dipping in enchilada sauce. Alternatively, on a microwave-safe plate, layer tortillas between moistened paper towels, cover with another moistened paper towel *(left)*, and microwave at the high setting for 40 seconds.

Mexican Pizza Supreme

In recent years, pizza lovers have learned that the popular pies can feature toppings that travel far beyond Italy. This version features a cheese-laced cornmeal crust, taco sauce, fresh vegetables, and chunks of veggie burger.

Preparation Time: 25 minutes I Total Time: 45 minutes I Servings: 8

½ cup plus 1 tablespoon yellow cornmeal

1½ cups all-purpose flour

2 teaspoons baking powder

¼ teaspoon salt

1 package (8 ounces/2 cups) shredded Colby Jack cheese

¾ cup nonfat milk

3 tablespoons vegetable oil

4 *Morningstar Farms Grillers Prime* Veggie Burgers

 - *or* -

4 other *Morningstar Farms* Veggie Burgers of your choice

1½ cups medium-hot taco sauce

¼ teaspoon garlic salt

1 medium green bell pepper, cut into rings, seeds and veins removed (about 1 cup)

½ cup chopped onion

½ cup sliced mushrooms

¼ cup sliced pitted black olives

For best results, see our tips on pages 8-9.

1. Preheat oven to 450°F. Coat 12-inch pizza pan with vegetable cooking spray. Sprinkle evenly with the 1 tablespoon cornmeal. Set aside.

2. In medium mixing bowl, combine ½ cup cornmeal, flour, baking powder, salt, and ½ cup of the cheese. Set aside. In another bowl, beat together milk and oil. Add to flour mixture, stirring only until combined. Press dough evenly into prepared pizza pan, pinching edges to form rim. Bake in preheated oven until lightly browned, about 10 minutes.

3. While crust is baking, break veggie burgers into small bite-sized pieces and put in mixing bowl with taco sauce and garlic salt. Stir well to coat burger pieces with sauce and seasoning. Spread mixture evenly over hot crust. Arrange green pepper rings, onion, mushrooms, and olives on top and spread evenly with remaining cheese. Return to oven and bake until sauce is bubbly and cheese has melted, 10 minutes longer. Serve hot, cut into 8 slices.

NUTRITION FACTS: Serving Size: 1 Slice; Calories: 390; Calories from Fat: 160; Total Fat: 18g; Saturated Fat: 7g; Cholesterol: 26mg; Sodium: 760mg; Total Carbohydrates: 36g; Dietary Fiber: 4g; Sugars: 3g; Protein: 20g.

Veggie Burger Pizza Variations

Using a homemade cornmeal crust like the one in the recipe above, or a ready-to-use store-bought pizza crust, it's easy to come up with all kinds of different pizzas with your own favorite veggie burgers, along with your choice of pizza sauce, pesto sauce or salsa; cut-up fresh vegetables; and shredded cheeses. For a Spicy Black Bean Pizza *(right)*, thaw and dice 4 *Morningstar Farms* Spicy Black Bean Burgers. Evenly spread them on a 12-ounce prepared pizza crust along with ½ cup chopped onion, ½ cup tomato salsa, and ¼ cup chopped cilantro. Top with 4 ounces packaged shredded pizza cheese and bake in a 450°F oven until the cheese has melted, 12 to 14 minutes.

Barbecue Hash

Hash recipes traditionally make smart use of leftovers, which are chopped up, seasoned, and heated together. Here, the only leftovers might be boiled potatoes, cut up along with other vegetables and veggie burgers to make a great one-dish meal. Feel free to add other veggies. Or try other one-skillet veggie burger variations (see sidebar).

Preparation Time: 30 minutes | Total Time: 40 minutes | Servings: 6

4 *Morningstar Farms Grillers* Original Veggie Burgers

 - or -

4 other *Morningstar Farms* Veggie Burgers of your choice

1 cup chopped onion

1 cup chopped green bell pepper

1 cup chopped red bell pepper

1 tablespoon vegetable oil

4 cups cubed cooked potatoes

¾ cup bottled barbecue sauce

¼ teaspoon salt

¼ teaspoon black pepper

For best results, see our tips on pages 8-9.

1. Cut veggie burgers into small bite-sized pieces. Set aside.

2. In large skillet, sauté onion and green and red bell peppers in oil over medium heat. When they start to become tender, stir in potatoes, veggie burgers, barbecue sauce, salt, and pepper.

3. Simmer hash mixture, stirring occasionally, until thoroughly heated, about 10 minutes. Serve immediately.

NUTRITION FACTS: Serving Size: I cup; Calories: 285; Calories from Fat: 80; Total Fat: 9g; Saturated Fat: Ig; Cholesterol: 0mg; Sodium: 400mg; Total Carbohydrates: 37g; Dietary Fiber: 4g; Sugars: 4g; Protein: 13g.

Another Great Skillet Supper Idea

To make an easy Western Bean Skillet that serves 6, sauté I cup chopped green bell pepper and I cup chopped onion in 2 teaspoons vegetable oil in a nonstick skillet until tender. Stir in 2 cans (28 ounces each) vegetarian baked beans; 4 finely chopped veggie burgers of your choice or a package of *Morningstar Farms Meal Starters Grillers* Recipe Crumbles; ½ cup hot-and-spicy barbecue sauce; ¼ cup firmly packed dark brown sugar; and I½ teaspoons dry mustard. Bring to a boil, reduce heat, and simmer, uncovered, for 5 minutes, stirring frequently. Serve sprinkled with chopped tomato and chopped fresh parsley, if desired.

Tabbouleh-style Couscous

Take a dinnertime trip to the eastern Mediterranean without ever leaving home, with the help of a veggie burger recipe featuring the tiny grain-shaped North African pasta known as couscous. It's prepared here in the style of the traditional Lebanese grain dish called tabbouleh.

Preparation Time: 20 minutes | Total Time: 20 minutes | Servings: 4

4 *Morningstar Farms* Grillers Original Veggie Burgers

 - or -

4 other *Morningstar Farms* Veggie Burgers of your choice

1⅓ cups canned vegetable broth

2 cloves garlic, minced

1 cup quick-cooking couscous *(see sidebar, below)*

1½ cups chopped tomatoes

⅔ cup sliced green onions

¼ cup slivered fresh basil leaves

3 tablespoons lemon juice

2 tablespoons chopped fresh mint leaves

4 teaspoons olive oil

¼ teaspoon black pepper

⅓ cup crumbled reduced-fat feta cheese

For best results, see our tips on pages 8-9.

1. Cook veggie burgers according to package directions.

2. Meanwhile, in medium saucepan, bring broth and garlic to a boil. Stir in couscous. Remove pan from heat. Cover and let stand until liquid is absorbed, about 5 minutes.

3. In large bowl combine couscous mixture, tomatoes, onions, basil, lemon juice, mint, oil, and pepper. Spoon onto 4 serving plates. Top each with warm burger, broken or cut into bite-sized pieces. Sprinkle with feta cheese. Serve immediately.

NUTRITION FACTS: Serving Size: 1⅛ cups; Calories: 400; Calories from Fat: 110; Total Fat: 13g; Saturated Fat: 2.5g; Cholesterol: 5mg; Sodium: 750mg; Total Carbohydrates: 45g; Dietary Fiber: 6g; Sugars: 4g; Protein: 24g.

Preparing Instant Couscous

Many people who've enjoyed the North African specialty called couscous think it's a special kind of grain. In fact, it's a tiny pasta shape made from wheat flour, like other more familiar pastas, although couscous is steamed in a way similar to rice or other grains. Traditional couscous steams for 30 minutes or longer. Fortunately, modern cooks can take advantage of packaged "instant" couscous, available in many supermarkets. Precooked and then re-dried, it requires only 5 minutes of rehydrating in boiling liquid. After cooking, however, all kinds of couscous benefit from being raked lightly with the tines of a fork *(right)* to separate the particles so the couscous will become fluffy and mix easily with other ingredients.

Green Bean Cheese Potato Pie

Convenient frozen hash browns become the crust for this imaginative and easy main-course pie filled with tasty veggie burger pieces. Feel free to substitute other frozen vegetables for the green beans, if you prefer.

Preparation Time: 20 minutes | Total Time: 40 minutes | Servings: 6

4 *Morningstar Farms*
Grillers Prime Veggie Burgers

- or -

4 other *Morningstar Farms*
Veggie Burgers of your choice

3 cups frozen shredded hash
browns, thawed

2 cups frozen French-cut
green beans

1 can (10¾ ounces)
Cheddar cheese soup

½ cup milk

1 can (2.8 ounces)
French-fried onions

½ teaspoon salt

¼ teaspoon black pepper

1 tablespoon Worcestershire sauce

½ cup shredded Cheddar cheese

*For best results, see our tips
on pages 8-9.*

1. Preheat oven to 450°F. Cut veggie burgers into small bite-sized pieces. Set aside.

2. Coat bottom and sides of 9-inch pie plate with vegetable cooking spray. Evenly line plate with hash browns. Bake until golden brown, about 25 minutes. Remove from oven and reduce oven temperature to 350°F.

3. In mixing bowl, combine veggie burgers, green beans, soup, milk, I cup of the onions, salt, pepper, and Worcestershire sauce. Spread mixture inside hot hash brown crust. Top with cheese and remaining ½ cup onions.

4. Bake until thoroughly heated through, about 20 minutes. Serve hot, spooned onto individual serving plates.

NUTRITION FACTS: Serving Size: I cup; Calories: 375; Calories from Fat: I70; Total Fat: I9g; Saturated Fat: 6g; Cholesterol: I6mg; Sodium: 870mg; Total Carbohydrates: 34g; Dietary Fiber: 4g; Sugars: Ig; Protein: I7g.

An Unusually Good Casserole Idea

Oven-baked casseroles are a terrific, easy way to prepare a heartwarming main course featuring veggie burgers. For an unusual and delicious Baked Chik Salad *(right)*, in a mixing bowl combine 4 *Morningstar Farms Chik Patties* Original, cut up into small bite-sized pieces, with 2 cups diced celery, I cup thawed frozen peas, ¼ cup diced pimiento, ¼ cup diced green pepper, and 2 tablespoons finely chopped onion. In another bowl, stir together I½ cups reduced-calorie mayonnaise, ½ cup shredded American cheese, I tablespoon lemon juice, and ¼ teaspoon salt; then, toss thoroughly with *Chik Patties* mixture. Coat shallow 2-quart casserole with vegetable cooking spray. Spread mixture inside and bake in preheated 350°F oven until thoroughly heated through, about 30 minutes. Sprinkle with I cup crushed potato chips, ½ cup additional shredded cheese, and bake until cheese melts, about I0 minutes longer. Serves 6.

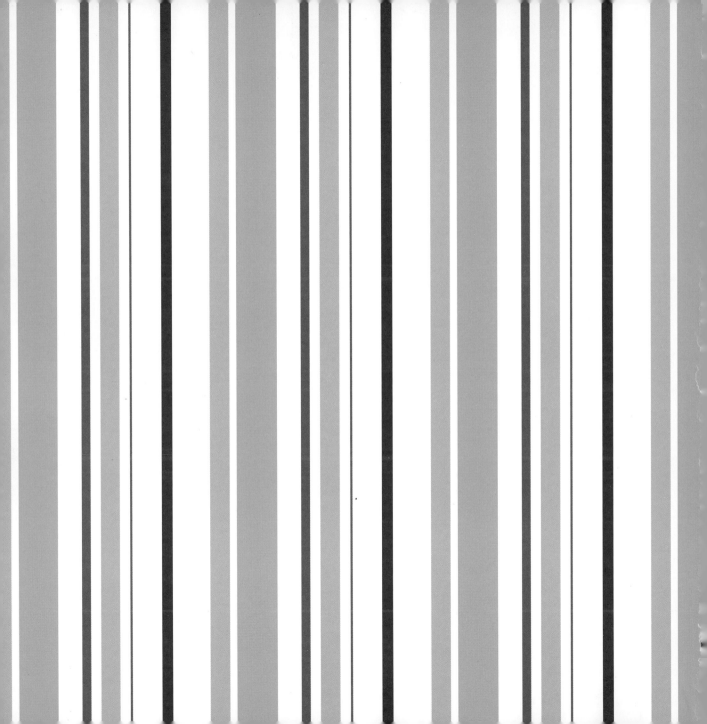